Criminal Defense Investigation

Theory, Practice, and Methods

by

I0442105

Jeremy Lee Pennington

Published by Pennington & Associates ltd.

www.pennassoc.com

Ironton, Ohio

ISBN-13: 978-1530614516

Dedicated To:

Allison Pennington

My loving wife, who tolerates my needless ranting of information, long work hours, and my obsessive quest for knowledge.

About the Author

Jeremy Pennington is the founder and owner of Pennington & Associates ltd., a private investigation and analysis firm specializing in criminal defense investigations. Mr. Pennington is a former U.S. Marine who served in the Military Police. He also served as a civilian in the federal service as a Federal Officer. He holds a master's degree in Intelligence Studies with a concentration in Analysis from American Public University System.

His current research involves investigative and analytical methodologies specific to criminal defense. Mr. Pennington is an Adjunct Professor of Criminal Justice.

Mr. Pennington welcomes any comments or critical feedback on the following work at Jpennington@pennassoc.com.

Table of Contents

Criminal Defense Investigation

Theory, Practice, and Methods

Introduction

This book specifically addresses the professional practice of criminal defense investigators. Although there are many aspects that could be addressed, this book's focus is on the analytical skills needed to undertake the endeavor of criminal defense investigations. There are many aspects of a criminal defense investigator's profession that the reader will still have questions about after finishing this book. These areas, however, are domain specific and therefore not the focus here. In many cases, this book describes these areas in general terms; however, it is not my intention to delve into specific domains of knowledge that deal with particular forensic issues and investigative tradecraft. An abundance of literature already exists on those topics, and any attempt to tackle them in this book would only be redundant and in vain.

Amongst all available literature on criminal investigations one thing is very apparent: there is a high degree of focus on collection methods. In simple terms, this means the practice of collecting information referred to as evidence. This may seem appropriate considering the purpose of a criminal investigations. However, this selective focus on information gathering has devastating consequences on the assessment and interpretation of the evidence uncovered through a criminal investigation. This book diverts from this main focus in the literature by drawing attention to the assessment and interpretation of evidence, not just its collection.

Including collection methodologies in this book may be appropriate, but it would also be redundant. Professional investigators, both public and private, have access to volumes of literature written on collection methods, the range of which covers witness interviews to the collection of physical evidence. Moreover, including collection methods within this book would offer only a limited view of specific areas; volumes would be needed to properly cover this material.

The analytical theory and skills required in criminal investigations, specifically in criminal defense investigations, represents an overwhelming gap in current literature. Many academics and working professionals would argue that methods of evidence analysis are covered; however, this is simply not true. For example, the available literature on analysis in forensic science has an extremely limited focus on results: the identification of blood, the matching of latent fingerprints, toxicology, and the list goes on. The resulting analysis is simply another form of evidence that must be incorporated into the overall reconstruction of past events. The criminal investigator, in the end, is left with the task of interpreting the final results of any given forensic process.

In order to fill this void in the literature, this book specifically addresses analytical methodologies and processes and is aimed at professional practicing criminal defense investigators. However, these same methodologies and processes are applicable to law enforcement investigations. In practice, the methods are the same no matter which side of the courtroom is presenting its results.

While drafting this book, considerable focus was given to the simplicity of its presentation. Although this book could have been written in a more technical format with considerable complexity, the end goal was that the material would be clear and easy to use. That said, many of the topics presented are complex. Unlike books that spend page after page trying to drive home a point through differing points of view, this book presents information from the perspective of what you need to know and not to prove a particular point. Many topics require the reader to obtain real life experience and apply the methods and practices presented in order to fully understand them. A reader of this book should consume the information and then, simply, put it into practice. Much like the concepts underpinning complex math, the information presented in this book requires effort on the part of the reader for full comprehension.

Part 1

Chapter 1

The Professional Criminal Defense Investigator

Criminal defense investigators are often considered (or perceived as) black hats by the public and licensed private investigators. The general public has little understanding of criminal defense investigations. Likewise, many licensed private investigators shun this practice due to a lack of understanding and, in many cases, moral objections. Criminal defense has been left to those with the courage and motivation to take on an endeavor that is unpopular and often socially taboo. It is an important undertaking in society. At times, the innocent are placed on trial and stand the liability of being stripped of life and liberty.

DNA testing and post-trial defense by the Innocence Project have allowed us to see many wrongly convicted individuals freed from incarceration. Many advocates of their prosecutions have been dismayed by their release, but there is an important lesson to learn from their exoneration: criminal defense investigators are a necessary and important aspect of the criminal trial process. They are just as essential as attorneys. The prosecution holds a legion of resources, chief among them is law enforcement, with a multi-tiered structure of investigators and other support. No state would remove this important resource from the hands of prosecutors. Why should a criminal defendant be denied the same resource? From the author's point of view, criminal defense investigation is one of the most pivotal issues in criminal defense.

The services of a criminal defense investigator are extremely valuable in defending the accused. A defense investigator is able to shed light on the "real terms" of an alleged incident. To a large degree, defense cases hold a veil of secrecy. The State presents a case of complete guilt and will vigorously hold this view unless dislodged from its position. A defense investigator is able to provide a stream of unbiased information to the defense attorney who is then able give weight to arguments. This unbiased information is obtained, to some extent, through the same process used by law enforcement, but it is objective.

Criminal defense is expensive, more so than most could fathom. From the author's experience, the cost of a defense for the accused can easily exceed $10,000 for a common case. This can easily double with the participation of a criminal defense investigator. Although a criminal defense investigator's hourly fees are normally less than those of an attorney, the time required to complete a criminal defense investigation is considerably more than the time invested by an experienced attorney in most cases. Thus, a full defense, comprised of an attorney and defense investigator, can make a considerable economic impact and in many cases is impossible for the defendant.

This issue of economic impact is only further enhanced when the social class of most criminal defendants is taken into account. Most criminal defendants are poor or would struggle to pay for a private defense. In turn, the State pays the bill. This process and the resources provided vary from jurisdiction to jurisdiction. Nevertheless, in many cases, the resource of a criminal defense investigator remains unseen in many defense cases.

In many jurisdictions, a criminal defense investigator's services are only called upon during the worst cases, such as rape or murder. This causes a stovepipe affect in the area of criminal defense investigation. With a low rate of use, the professional development of a criminal defense investigator can be slow. There is no clear development track to becoming a criminal defense investigator. There is no college degree available for mentorship and training. The sad reality is that there are simply no qualified criminal defense investigators available in many jurisdictions.

The background to practicing criminal defense investigation varies. Some investigators emerge from careers in reporting, law enforcement, or for-profit investigations. Regardless of their backgrounds, over time, many develop the necessary skills. In many cases, they were the only ones available and through trial by fire they branded themselves in this role.

There has been considerable debate among licensed private investigators as to the appropriate background for successfully gaining entry into the industry. Many licensed private investigators have shown extreme bias toward former law enforcement officers. This colorful discussion can sometimes be found online, and the same bias appears during public interviews when licensed private investigators are asked about the appropriate background for criminal defense investigators. However, this bias is normally exhibited by licensed private investigators who do not have a law enforcement background.

Critics of law enforcement officers becoming private investigators have cited an array of negative factors. Chief among them is that law enforcement officers tend to overwork assignments, exceed established budgets, lack any real business experience, use deplorable tactics, and hold an overwhelmingly dogmatic view of criminal defendants. On the other hand, these critics rarely recognize the investigative skills held by law enforcement officers. To a mild degree, these criticisms have some validity, but these arguments are almost always riddled with bias and driven by the need for personal branding in business.

Popular culture and Hollywood have branded the private investigation industry as corrupt and exemplified by distasteful investigative work. As with many professions, Hollywood has failed to capture the reality of the private investigation industry, presenting the main revenue generator as cases of infidelity. Unfortunately, this image has taken a stronghold in popular culture and has only been reinforced by true stories of corrupt and unskilled private investigators in the mainstream media. Today, the public views private investigators as individuals who operate in dark alleys while gathering negative information on otherwise innocent citizens.

Over the years, working private investigators have tried to polish their public image. However, these attempts have largely failed. In the same token, individual private investigators have used their qualifications as evidence of the quality service provided to the public at large. Those from a non-law enforcement background are met head on by public knowledge of and overwhelming familiarity with law enforcement officers. In turn, while promoting a professional image, the individual is confronted with public questions of credibility and skills. In simple terms, is a private investigator with no law enforcement experience really qualified to work as an agent for hire? Many different answers could be given in response to this question. However, those with no law enforcement background still perceive a need to defend their credentials. In necessitating this justification, the industry has cast a black cloud over those with law enforcement experience. In reality, individuals from a wide array of backgrounds could qualify to work as private investigators.

The obvious background for a criminal defense investigator is training in law enforcement; however, this logic is false. The person most qualified is someone trained and educated to work as a criminal defense investigator. Many professionals are trained in this same way. For example, physicians are trained in medical school and then mentored during a residency. Why should this be different for a criminal defense investigator? Unfortunately, there is no school of higher education for criminal defense investigators. Thus, most working professionals arrive from different occupations and few are trained through internships.

Investigator vs. Attorney

In the area of criminal defense, the criminal defense investigator and defense attorney are a team. However, there can be conflicts in this relationship that require special attention, which are noted within this book. The criminal defense investigator, in particular, can find navigating this relationship confusing at times.

The criminal defense attorney is the forefront in all matters. In simple terms, the attorney is the tip of the spear. Any criminal defense endeavor is only as strong as the attorney leading the defense. The criminal defense investigator plays a supporting role, comprised of gathering evidence, analyzing evidence, and serving as an expert witness. The investigator uncovers and analyzes information, known as evidence. How this evidence is used and argued in court is the responsibility of the criminal defense attorney.

In practice, this relationship can have overlaps at times. The criminal defense investigator must be attentive to these overlaps when they occur. In many cases they can detract from the investigator's work and in some cases will hinder the defense of the accused. An investigator should never give an opinion on a matter of law to a criminal defendant, or anyone for that matter. A criminal defense investigator is not an attorney. There are some investigators who are qualified to advise on legal matters because they have attended law school and are admitted to the bar. However, even in this case, the investigator should strictly avoid giving an opinion. Legal advice should be solely left to the criminal defense attorney, who holds the responsibility of representing the defendant. The only discussion of legal matters the investigator should have is directly with the responsible attorney, away from the defendant.

A criminal defense investigator should not attempt to formulate a defense strategy. The investigator should provide all available information and evidence to the defense attorney, who in turn will decide the specific defense strategy. This is a reoccurring issue with investigators working as law enforcement officers and criminal defense investigators, alike. An investigator should not be concerned with possible legal arguments in relation to evidence. The only opinion an investigator should hold and openly discuss is whether the collected evidence is credible. Credibility should be the foremost concern for any investigator, who holds the responsibility for collecting and documenting evidence. This responsibility is referred to as the "burden of proof," where the attorney has the "burden of argument."

Any relationship between an investigator and attorney will ultimately be driven by the personality of the responsible attorney. Views and work habits differ among attorneys. In light of this, the criminal defense investigator will need to conform to the needs and views of the attorney. This can be frustrating, but it is the reality of the profession. The only exception to this is when unethical conduct occurs. Unfortunately, there may be unethical attorneys who demand unethical conduct from criminal defense investigators. If this occurs, the criminal defense investigator should simply refuse the work, citing their objections.

Ethical and Moral Issues

Ethical and moral objections to criminal defense are all too common among private investigators and law enforcement officers. Society, through pop culture, views criminal proceedings in terms of good versus evil. This is also prevalent on the investigative level. Popular television shows such as *CSI*, *COPS*, NCIS, and many more have done nothing but promote this fantasy of a war against evil. In the author's experience, law enforcement has completely bought into this fantasy. This is not to say that reasonable and objective investigators do not exist within law enforcement; among the ranks of law enforcement, professional, objective investigators exist, but they are the minority. Unfortunately, many law enforcement cases are plagued by overwhelming bias. On the other hand, private investigators of limited backgrounds have also fallen into this fantasy.

The ethical and moral objections to criminal defense should be important to the criminal defense investigator. Many of these objections are held by most individuals and are rooted not in popular culture but in religious and personal views. These moral or ethical objections can be a considerable stumbling block to an effective investigation. The importance of an ethical framework becomes paramount in the criminal defense investigator's professional work.

Bias is something that all persons experience in their daily lives. A criminal defense investigator is no exception. However, in the case of a criminal defense investigator, bias comes at an extreme cost. Moral or ethical objections to a crime are of little concern during a criminal defense investigation. This is not saying criminal defense investigators have released themselves from any moral or ethical obligations. In reality, a criminal defense investigator must have a well-grounded ethical and moral framework, but it must be separated from bias-driven accusations of an alleged criminal.

Morally and ethically, crime is wrong. In the same light, false statements, material misrepresentations, and empty arguments brought against the accused are also morally and ethically wrong, to the same degree. Unfortunately, these moral and ethical violations are all too common in our criminal justice system. The criminal defense investigator's purpose and ethical obligation is to provide an objective assessment of witness statements, evidence, and the overall credibility of criminal allegations.

Unlike the criminal defense attorney, the criminal defense investigator is not an advocate. The temptation of holding an opinion regarding the accused's guilt or innocence should be avoided. A criminal defense investigator should not speak or think in these terms. For the criminal defense investigator, determining guilt or innocence should be solely left to the court. Instead, the investigator should take a view grounded in fact and based upon what is known with a high degree of probability, which is determined through objective investigation.

The formation of bias is rooted in the interpretation of evidence. In terms of a criminal defense investigation, there is a critical difference between interpretation and analysis. Interpretation, in simple terms, is the action of judgement, which is the responsibility of the court. On the other hand, analysis is the action of viewing any one incident from an array of perspectives and not making a judgement but uncovering all available evidence to aid the court in judgement. A criminal defense investigator does not interpret evidence. The concern, from the perspective of the criminal defense investigator, is not the issue of guilt or innocence but uncovering all evidence and assessing its credibility.

In practice, a criminal defense investigator is responsible for providing unbiased information to the criminal defense attorney. This task can be easily misunderstood, but it holds great importance ethically, morally, and professionally. The opposing side, the State, will only provide evidence of guilt to the court, and in many cases, this evidence will be rife with bias. This bias comes in one of two forms: the denial of evidence that would cast a doubt on the alleged guilt and evidence that is of questionable credibility. The criminal defense investigator counters this bias through object analysis.

An in-depth examination of the adversarial process that plays out in the courtroom and within the hallways of the courthouse will lead any reasonable person to determine that assessing the guilt or innocence of the accused is dangerous for any criminal defense investigator. The objectivity of the criminal defense investigator is the foundation of an ethical and moral framework. Otherwise, only a biased work product will be produced, and the risk of a truly innocent person losing their freedom becomes more likely.

Beyond a "perspective grounded in fact," a criminal defense investigator has other professional ethical obligations. These are not morally based but have been developed by the legal profession. In general, criminal defense investigators, or licensed private investigators more broadly, do not have a generally accepted ethical code of professional conduct. The writings of licensed private investigators focus strongly on the detailed tradecraft of investigations but overall do not address ethical professional conduct in any real detail. This creates a critical void for any investigator who enters the courtroom or whose work product finds its way into the court's view. The current standard, which will most likely remain, is the Professional Code of Responsibility adhered to by attorneys. When a licensed private investigator is retained by an attorney or whose work product is assessed by a court of law, the Professional Code of Responsibility adhered to by attorneys will most likely come to bare on the evidence uncovered by the licensed private investigator. In this same light, a criminal defense investigator, in most case an independent licensed private investigator, must adhere to the same ethical standards as an attorney.

The Professional Code of Responsibility can vary from state to state. Generally, the ethical requirements of each state should model the framework of the America Bar

Association's Center for Professional Responsibility.[1] Within the American Bar Association's Model Rules of Professional Conduct, there are several areas a criminal defense investigator should be familiar with and strictly adhere too.

The model rules strictly prohibit criminal acts, and "conduct involving dishonesty, fraud, deceit or misrepresentation."[2] The prohibition of criminal acts pertains to the moral and ethical conduct of the criminal defense investigator. To some extent, the same could be said for issues of dishonesty, fraud, deceit, or misrepresentation. However, in the tradecraft of investigation, these can occur easily. Investigators typically employ deceit and misrepresentation through the use of pretexts, personal legends, and flat-out lies to gain access to information or elicit statements from parties who would otherwise avoid contact with an investigator. These tactics are well known among licensed private investigators and are probably employed daily within the industry. However, a criminal defense investigator must be beyond reproach in this area. There can be strictly no use of dishonesty, fraud, deceit, or misrepresentation in the conduct of the criminal defense investigator.

At first glance, many licensed private investigators would cringe at the idea of being stripped of the tools of deceit or misrepresentation. However, a criminal defense investigator's work must be completely overt. When a witness, law enforcement officer, or related party is contacted, they must be fully advised who the criminal defense investigator represents and in which criminal proceedings. There can simply be no misrepresentation of identity or fact.

Mindset

The mindset of a criminal defense investigator is of considerable importance. Mindset is the first and primary obstacle to working as a successful criminal defense investigator. In general, one's mindset has to be completely disconnected from the defendant's guilt or

---

[1] Model Rules of Professional Conduct. Americanbar.org, American Bar Association, Center for Professional Responsibility, 2013.

[2] Ibid.

innocence. This can be a considerable obstacle for former law enforcement officers entering the profession of for-profit criminal defense investigation. Thinking about "the good guys" (the cops) versus the "bad guys" (the accused), i.e., those accused by the "good guys," can have detrimental effects on the criminal defense investigator's work product. To a lesser degree, this same mindset can come into play with individuals from different former professions. If a criminal defense investigator does not eliminate this bias from their mindset, a biased work product will result and a wrongful conviction becomes more likely.

Qualifications of a Criminal Defense Investigator

The following are general guidelines for the qualifications of a criminal defense investigator:

1. Properly licensed in the jurisdiction of practice

2. Highly experienced in investigative field operations

3. A formal education at no less than the bachelor's level, however, a graduate level degree is preferred. A strong focuses on critical thinking, problem solving, and research should core to academic study.

4. Strong written and verbal communication skills cannot be overly stressed

5. Working knowledge of the 4th and 5th Amendments

6. Working knowledge of law enforcement procedures and applied practices as they relate to the full spectrum of criminal investigations

7. For the proper and successful performance of criminal defense investigations, the investigator must have specialized experience in the following areas in order to comprehensively complete a criminal defense investigation:

    1. A fundamental understanding of the full spectrum of criminal acts as they relate to the criminal defense investigator's specific practice

    2. Highly developed interview skills

    3. Public records research skills

    4. Forensic photography skills

    5. Ability to reconstruct crime scenes

6. Evidence collection and preservation techniques

7. Structured analysis methods

8. Counterintelligence

9. General social knowledge

Chapter 2

Defining Investigation

The term "investigation" is used in specific academic endeavors and professional pursuits. Society has incorporated this term to define many professions. For example, we have investigative journalists, criminal investigators, and individuals conducting investigations into matters pertaining to academia, medicine, politics, history; the list reaches the furthest segments of society. The term "investigation" is likely one of the most overly used terms in connection with human pursuits, to the extent that its meaning has become generic and is applied to promote the endeavor's professionalism or the end work product as more credible than one not produced by "investigation." In reality, many times there has not been a true investigation but rather an opinion-forming endeavor that is riddled with bias. The ambiguity of the term "investigation" is a critical issue in the context of a criminal defense investigator's work.

A professional criminal defense investigator cannot view an investigation through ambiguity. A criminal defense investigation must be definable through a specific framework. A criminal defense investigation and a criminal investigation are one and the same. The difference is the purpose of the investigator, one of criminal defense and one of criminal prosecution. However, regardless of the investigator's purpose, several key questions emerge when attempting to define an "investigation." Is an investigation a scientific pursuit? Is it a matter of tradecraft utilized to uncover unknown information? Is an investigation a simple search for the truth? Many questions could be posed, but these are the core questions in defining the term "investigation" in the context of a criminal defense investigation.

Conducting an investigation is a scientific endeavor. The core concept in the scientific method is the generation of a hypothesis and deriving results from testing the hypothesis. Theories are formulated upon the results that are found true to the degree of repeatability.[3] In general, the scientific method is an investigation in scientific terms. Is it applicable to the work of a criminal defense investigator? To a large degree, it is.

In many aspects of a criminal defense investigator's work the scientific method will be utilized. For example, a defendant allegedly traveled from a known location and then arrived at another known location at an approximate time. This allegation can be viewed as a hypothesis and tested. The distances can be traveled by the alleged means and timed. The allegation, the hypothesis, is tested providing a result that can be repeated by another party to confirm its credibility. Thus, the scientific method is utilized to prove or disprove the allegation.

The scientific method is dominant in the forensic sciences. The use of forensic methods has become commonplace in criminal investigations. Some forensic methods could be consider pseudo-science, considering their subjective nature. However, forensic methods, derived from the hard sciences of chemistry, biology, and material engineering, have a solid foundation rooted in the scientific method. In many cases, the criminal defense investigator will utilize forensic methods personally or use the results of forensic lab reporting.

Even though the application of the scientific method holds considerable utility in criminal defense investigations, its application is limited in the traditional sense. In general, the criminal defense investigator must reconstruct an alleged incident of criminal behavior in the past. The scientific method is only applicable to a hypothesis that can be tested using an experiment in the present. A criminal defense investigator is therefore faced with assessing

---

[3] "What Is the ``Scientific Method"?." Physics.Ucr.Edu. Accessed October 10, 2015. http:// physics.ucr.edu/~wudka/Physics7/Notes_www/node6.html.

a hypothesis grounded in human action that occurred in the past. Facets of this historical event can be fully assessed in a contemporary setting, for example, the previous example of a defendant traveling between two locations. On the other hand, some evidence will have been degraded by the passage of time and human deceit, or the original setting cannot be recreated for experimentation with any real degree of certainty. As a result, the traditional scientific method will not be useful in all circumstances. In many cases, a hypothesis simply cannot be tested. The formulation of the hypothesis is possible, but the testing of that hypothesis may be impossible. For example, a criminal defense investigator is able to test the ability of an eyewitness to have observed an incident through a vision study, but the content of the alleged observation is untestable. The criminal defense investigator is simply at the mercy of the witness's testimony.

The endeavor of reconstructing a historical event may lay squarely beyond the scope of the scientific method. Proof of this is found in the existence of both law enforcement investigators and forensic investigators. If all crimes could be solved through the traditional scientific method, law enforcement investigators would be long extinct. This brings the core investigative methods used by criminal investigators into focus.

Investigation is tradecraft. Criminal investigation is largely based upon the uncovering evidence of guilt through the exploitation of human sources. Through interviewing witnesses and interrogating suspects, criminal investigators are able to essentially fill the void left by the shortcomings of the scientific method or limited resources. Many working professionals and academics would argue that this process, or cluster of methods, is based upon sound research and is the result of professional training. However, history paints a very different image. The tradecraft of handling and exploiting human sources has a long, rich history largely ignored by contemporary practitioners. What is practiced today was already well known in the 1800s. The exploitation of human sources goes well beyond the concept of asking questions during an interview or interrogation and includes the use of undercover operatives, informers, and social engineering. These concepts are still applied in the same fashion in the present, except where limited by the law.

A detailed examination of the scientific method coupled with historical tradecraft reveals a gap in the overall process of completing an investigation. In many cases, practitioners will refer to initiative reasoning or logical reasoning while citing their experiences in dealing with similar matters to fill this gap. Another common analogy used to explain this process or fill the gap is "connecting the dots." However, no real explanation is given on how this process occurs. Connecting the dots is by far the most unexplained aspect of completing an investigation regarding criminal activity. The absence of explanation bring many questions into focus in regard to what a "criminal investigation" specifically is or is not. In reality, investigators have been historically left to their own devices in this area.

The author's experience as a law enforcement officer and criminal defense investigator suggests that the process of "connecting the dots" is relatively simplistic in its historical application and as the driving force of any investigation. Generally, information is initially collected during the early stages of the investigation. This process is normally conducted by the first responders to the alleged crime, typically patrol officers. In some cases, the initial response will be made by detectives, but this would be unusual. Following the initial collection of information, an investigation is initiated in a formalized process where a detective, also referred to as a criminal investigator, or a group of detectives assumes responsibility for investigating the alleged crime. "Leads" will be generated based upon a review of the initial information collected by the first responders of the alleged crime. The term "lead" is generic and refers to information utilized in the attempt to generate additional information. For example, during an interview with a witness, the witness states that two other people were present during the alleged crime. These two possible witnesses were previously unknown. As a result, this new information is considered a "lead," and the two individuals would be interviewed, resolving the lead or generating additional leads based upon their statements. "Resolving" the lead refers to being unable to generate any additional information and is sometimes referred to as a "dead lead." However, in the context of the term "lead," any number of possible information sources could be targeted for additional information. The generation of leads could cause an investigator to examine a location, person, or any other information source. In theory, as many leads as possible are generated until no more additional leads can be generated. After completing this process, the investigation is closed through the arrest of an individual, or the case is considered "cold," referring to the inability to generate any additional leads. Terms used to describe this process will vary depending on the local slang used by investigator. Moreover, law enforcement agencies will also use formalized terms specific to case closure and non-closure to describe the end results of an investigation. However, no matter the terminology used, the underpinning concepts are the same. This process, in traditional terms, is the concept of "connecting the dots" from the perspective of a criminal investigator. For clarity, this process is best termed "investigating through lead generation."

The concepts presented in this book are not meant to challenge the process of investigating through lead generation but rather build upon this concept. Simply stated, this book focuses on "connecting the dots" from the perspective of a criminal defense investigator, although the same concepts presented in this book should be applied by criminal investigators. To fully understand the concepts presented throughout this book, a different definition of the term "investigation" is needed.

The initial description of "investigation" focused on the scientific method coupled with historical investigation tradecraft methods through lead generation. Simply stated, this overall investigative process is like attempting to see through muddy water. The process is abstract and lacks a clear conceptual framework.

In this book, "investigation" is defined through two clearly defined segments, which represent two codependent processes. The first segment is referred to as "collection." This is the process of collecting information. Collection entails many traditional tradecraft methods used by criminal investigators and has traditionally been the primary focus of criminal investigations. The second segment is referred to as "analysis." This term describes the task of processing, deconstructing, visualizing, and conducting diagnostic testing of information. To a limited degree, analysis entails the scientific method. However, the analytical methods presented in this book go beyond what is known as the scientific method by their ability to provide insight were the traditional scientific method fails. Traditionally, criminal investigations have held an overly simplistic focus of analysis at the initiative level. In this book, the coupled processes of "collection" and "analysis" are used to define the term "investigation." Both processes must be present to consider an endeavor an investigation.

Chapter 3

The Concept of Evidence

The main subject of any criminal defense investigator's daily work is evidence. The need for evidence is why attorneys hire criminal defense investigators. Considering its underpinning aspects, evidence is a complex subject. This is true in both civil and criminal litigation. The subject of evidence can be viewed from two differing perspectives: first, through a consideration of why some information is consider evidence and other information is not and second, through a consideration of what evidence really is and how it is used to define a subject under question.

Critical Thinking

The criminal defense investigator's primary task throughout any investigation is critical thinking. Beyond witness interviews and the overwhelming work of reviewing discovery material, the investigator is left with thought alone. Effective critical thinking skills differentiate a successful criminal defense investigator from one who will ultimately seek another niche in the for-profit investigations industry. A close examination of critical thinking reveals it to be a complex process of avoiding cognitive bias and stretching the imagination beyond first impressions.

Critical thinking emerges in three different forms: inductive, deductive, and abductive. All three forms overlap to some degree. Critical thinking in practice is a combination of all three forms in the development of "analytical beliefs."[4]

Inductive reasoning refers to generalization. This reasoning accounts for an array of possibilities but equally weights each possibility. In simple terms, this approach incorporates all possibilities and does not favor a specific one.[5] Deductive reasoning differs from inductive reasoning regarding generalization. Instead, deductive reasoning focuses on a specific possibility, eliminating other possibilities based on the information available. In the end, a single, final possibility is favored.[6] The pitfall of this form of reasoning is the risk of deception. The investigator's judgements can be anticipated, and misleading information can cause the investigator to reach an incorrect judgement. Abductive reasoning, in essence, is a combination of inductive and deductive reasoning, moving from generalizations or specifics to an array of possibilities weighted unequally. In simple terms, abductive reasoning examines all possibilities creating "novel means of explanation,"[7] thus reaching the most likely conclusion.

There is no doubt that critical thinking is a complex process rife with the risk of failure. As less-than-rational individuals, we construct a simplified model of the world around us to deal with a highly complex reality. As a result, we then "behave rationally within" our simplified view of reality.[8] A criminal defense investigator is faced with this very process of simplifying reality. We may advocate for the defendant, or we may fail to benefit the defendant. In either case, simplifying the process of investigation for us as criminal defense

---

[4] Moore, David T. Critical Thinking and Intelligence Analysis: Occasional Paper Number Fourteen. National Defense Intelligence College, 2007., p. 3

[5] Ibid., p. 4

[6] Ibid.

[7] Ibid.

[8] Heuer, Richards J. Psychology of Intelligence Analysis. Center for the Study of Intelligence, 1999., p. 3

investigators. From one of the two positions, we can simplify the overall process. This is the most generalized example of simplification but nevertheless illustrates it. The "tendency of people to perceive what they expect to perceive is more important than any tendency to perceive what they want to perceive."[9] Thus, our perception is a critical element in assessing information.

We make judgements based upon our perception of reality. How do we see reality? In general, individual perception of reality will vary depending on a person's background, education, and cultural foundation. For example, most law enforcement officers may perceive themselves as the "good guys." In turn, a law enforcement officer may see anyone who resists their authority and judgements as a "bad guy." In this view, all members of the defense are "bad guys," criminal defense investigators included! This perception of the "good guys" versus the "bad guys" is a prime example of simplification. The process of simplification is further strengthened through mental shortcuts.

We process information daily, and in doing so we tend to make mental shortcuts. These mental shortcuts are referred to as "heuristics." One of the most important heuristics is the "availability heuristic."[10] Simply stated, the availability heuristic is when individuals predict the probability of something based upon the most immediately available example. For example, you assume a task is easily completed because everyone you know has completed the task with ease. You base this judgment on available information or events you have observed. The representative heuristic entails processing information that you are familiar with, as a consequence leading you to misjudge the information. For example, if you observe a dirty person walking down the street carrying a large bag, you would most likely assume the person is homeless, unless you are aware of information to the contrary. The label of "homeless" is the most available example for you to interpret your observations of the

---

[9] Ibid., p. 9

[10] Cottam, Martha L., Beth Dietz-Uhler, Elena Mastors, and Thomas Preston. Introduction to Political Psychology. 2nd ed. New York: Psychology Press, 2010., p. 39-42

person. This is a simple example of how familiarity can be misleading and cause an error in judgement.

A criminal defense investigator must avoid all possible forms of bias. The concepts and methods presented in this book are specifically intended to uncover critical information that is often hidden in bias. A criminal defense investigator must be in constant pursuit of overcoming bias in order to enable objective results.

Understanding Information as Evidence

The perception and context of evidence used during an investigation is key. At times, the perception and context will be simple, and at other times they will be highly complex. In general, perception and context are used during an investigation to uncover the truth or understand what may be believed as the truth with a given degree of certainty. A given degree of certainty is a key aspect in any form of analysis during an investigation. In reality, the truth during any investigation is an abstract theoretical concept. In simple terms, truth does not exist.

During any investigation, the investigator can present evidence but can never present the truth with absolute, one-hundred percent certainty. The professional investigator is left viewing the investigation through a theoretical lens based on degrees of certainty. In the end, any professional investigator will finish an investigation with a low, high, or inconclusive degree of certainty, but the absolute truth will always remain elusive.

Evidence is a term used to define the proof of a theory or argument. In simple terms, evidence is based on perception. An item or event is evidence because we perceive it as evidence. Based on what is perceived as evidence, individuals make judgements using their "bias, distortions, uninformed logic, or downright prejudiced views."[11]   Determining something to be evidence is based on the viewer's perception of reality. Evidence is not truth; it is a fragment of the truth, a fragment that perceptions rest upon. Perceptions are directly

---

11 Elder, Richard Paul and Linda. The Miniature Guide to Critical Thinking: Concepts & Tools, 2006. http://www.criticalthinking.org/files/Concepts_Tools.pdf., p.4

tied to how the investigator perceives evidence and the context in which the evidence is examined. Beyond all technical terminology, evidence is simply information that is known and considered to define a specific phenomenon.

The Evidence Approach and Context Model

The terms "approach" and "context" deal directly with how the criminal defense investigator systematically responds to alleged evidence and the context from which the evidence is perceived. In simple terms, approach and context pertain to how evidence is interacted with in a given environment and how the evidence is perceived. Fortunately, we have a clear model to work from, which is depicted in Figure 4.1.

The model represents the perception and context used in a criminal defense investigator's analysis. The model is a high-level framework used as a theoretical lens. In general, the model represents how evidence should be perceived and processed from the perspective of making analytical judgments during an investigation.

Figure 4.1. Evidence Perception and Context Model

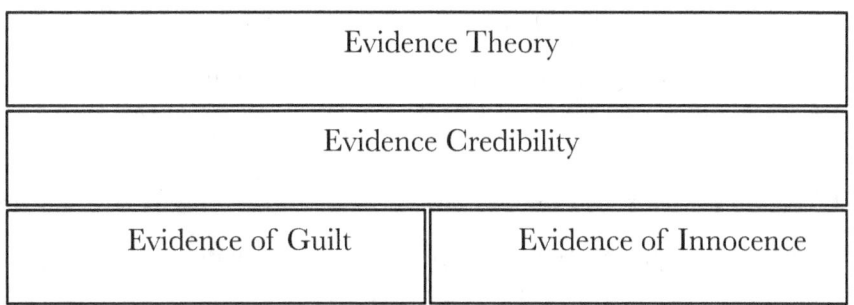

This model's foundation is comprised of evidence from the perspective of guilt and innocence. Evidence credibility and evidence theory are built upon this initial evidence. In simple terms, this model can be understood using the concept of building blocks. The foundation must exist before any additional blocks can be built on top of it. During the entire investigative process, evidence is repeatedly collected, processed, and interpreted through the Evidence Perception and Context Model.

To fully understand the theoretical lens employed within this model, and to further refine the structured analytical techniques embedded in it, several key terms must be defined. These terms are useful for processing and understanding the spectrum of evidence encountered during an investigation.

Evidence of innocence is simply defined as evidence proving the innocence of the accused. Evidence of guilt proves the accused is guilty of an alleged crime. Both forms of evidence are refined through evidence credibility, which is defined as the degree of belief in a specific facet of evidence. An evidence theory, or an Alternative Evidence Theory from the criminal defense investigator's view, is defined as the available competing views of a specific evidence's support for an array of possible criminal theories supporting innocence or guilt. Evidence of innocence, evidence of guilt, and the Alternative Evidence Theory are utilized to identify, collect, process, and interpret alleged evidence during the investigation of an alleged crime.

Understanding and identifying the difference between Evidence of innocence and Evidence of guilt is a complex and rigorous process. Unfortunately, historically this process has been based on initiative reasoning, which is prone to error. To fully evaluate the worth of specific evidence in proving innocence or guilt, more in-depth perception and context must be utilized, beyond simplistic intuitive reasoning. The credibility and theoretical interpretation of specific evidence has to be taken into account.

Evidence credibility is impacted by a wide array of factors. Credibility of evidence can range from low confidence to high confidence. The factors impacting this range vary depending on the type of evidence, which can include information gathered from deceptive witnesses and improperly collected or preserved physical evidence. From the perspective of the criminal defense investigator, evidence credibility is of special importance during a criminal defense investigation. The grim reality is that some evidence brought forth by the State has a low confidence level, for example, a witness providing incriminating testimony against a defendant based upon observations made during low-light conditions. How credible are the witness's observations? The criminal defense investigator has the responsibility of not only identifying this low confidence but also uncovering evidence that proves the specific evidence is of low quality. In terms of the above example, the criminal defense investigator would conduct a vision study to determine the quality of the witness's observation in the low-light environment. Evidence credibility is a key factor in any criminal defense investigation.

The Alternative Evidence Theory is based upon the perceptions of the observer and in many cases, upon close examination, will support a wide array of possibilities. In simple terms, the concept behind the Alternative Evidence Theory is that a facet of evidence can represent opposing interpretations or even any number of interpretations. For example, a fingerprint found on a murder victim's body can represent two opposing interpretations. The fingerprint is either the byproduct of the murderer touching the victim, or it represents the intimate touch of the victim's romantic lover. Thus, a specific facet of evidence can support more than one interpretation.

The Alternative Evidence Theory is the foundation of the criminal defense investigator's work. Generating an Alternative Evidence Theory is no simple task. A casual observer will most likely easily generate an alternative theory for specific evidence regarding the event in question. However, a layman's attempt is typically substandard and collapses easily under scrutiny. A holistic approach is required to adequately generate an Alternative Evidence Theory. To enable a holistic approach, evidence is placed in three categories: evidence, silent evidence, and absent evidence.

The first category, "evidence," incorporates all known information related to a specific phenomenon or, simply stated, an event. This information can vary wildly in form from witness testimony to physical evidence. Nevertheless, evidence is the information available for use in defining a specific event. For the criminal defense investigator, an event equals an alleged crime. The use of a specific facet of information used to define an event will vary depending on the bias or objective of the consumer of the information. For example, there will be differences in the ways the same information is used by the prosecutor and the defense attorney. Both parties will utilize the information to define the event in direct relation to their end goal of proving guilt or innocence. However, viewed holistically, the information defines the event and demonstrates what is known of the event.

The second category, "silent evidence," pertains to information that is unknown. This is a complex issue experienced during most investigations. Simply stated, silent evidence represents information that has not been discovered and may never be discovered. It cannot be utilized to make any form of judgement and essentially represents a true unknown facet of an event. For example, during a rape investigation, the State fails to collect biological material from the alleged crime scene, specifically, the bed sheets. This alleged rape occurred days before the alleged victim made the allegation. The bed sheets represent silent evidence because no information is known regarding the biological material that may or may not have existed on the bed sheets. The most critical issue with silent evidence is the inability to confirm its existence. If the criminal defense investigator could confirm the existence or nonexistence of the information, it would no longer silent evidence; it's proven existence would make it "evidence," and its proven nonexistence would make it "absent evidence."

The third category, "absent evidence," is a theoretical form of evidence largely overlooked by novice investigators. Simply stated, absent evidence is information that in theory should exist but does not exist. Why is this form of evidence theoretical? For absent evidence to exist an incorrect theory must be proposed. For example, for an act of theft to have occurred, items of value must be unaccounted for. The missing items of value are directly tied to the theory of theft. If no items were unaccounted for, would a theory of theft withstand scrutiny? No, because the existence of the items of value is the "absent evidence" needed for the theory of theft. The concept of absent evidence can be challenging to apply during complex investigations. The key is to determine specifically what information should exist and then confirm its nonexistence. If it is confirmed, then the information is silent evidence.

Investigative Evidentiary Equation

From an investigative evidentiary standpoint, and event can be described using the Investigative Evidentiary Equation:

Event = Evidence + Silent Evidence - Absent Evidence - Credibility

The Investigative Evidentiary Equation defines an event using a holistic approach. All forms of evidence are considered and are interdependent. How does one from of evidence impact another? This is a critical question for understanding how information defines an event. "Evidence" is known information, and "silent evidence" is unknown information. "absent evidence" is an indicator of a theoretical error in judgement. Credibility is not a form of evidence but is a reflection of just how real the information is or, simply stated, whether the information actually exists in the context presented. Combined, these variables define the full spectrum of knowledge regarding a specific event. All known information collectively is the foundation of knowledge of a specific event. Silent evidence represents the gaps in this knowledge. From a practical standpoint, silent evidence is information that could prove our belief wrong, known as the unforeseen. In turn, silent evidence is always a lingering issue during any investigation and is directly tied to the need for an investigation. Absent evidence is negative information that reduces the degree of certainty of known information when placed in context of the event as a whole.

Evidence credibility is a negative aspect that addresses specific facets of information, for example, specific physical evidence or a single segment of witness testimony. Evidence credibility is not evidence but rather a reflection of how the information actually exists in the context presented. For example, is a specific witness providing false information? What degree of certainty exists in the witness testimony as presented? These are common questions asked when determining the credibility of a witness's testimony. In practice, all information is considered credible unless some information exists that calls that credibility into question. Thus, a negative is created in the overall information spectrum defining the subject event.

The holistic approach of the Investigative Evidentiary Equation is based on known information, or evidence. Silent evidence, unknown information, is added to the known information. The sum of these defines an event. Absent evidence acts as a negative factor in defining the event. The key to understanding this evidence equation is that evidence and silent evidence will always exist; absent evidence will only exist during analytical errors in judgment. Evidence credibility is only a factor when information exists that creates a question of credibility. Evidence and silent evidence are the core information. Absent evidence and evidence credibility only address the interpretation of evidence and silent evidence. This is why absent evidence and evidence credibility act as negative factors in the Investigative Evidentiary Equation.

Silent evidence is key to understanding the Alternative Evidence Theory. How can the sum of evidence, the known information, and silent evidence, the unknown information, define an event? Moreover, how does this concept have any utility in a criminal defense investigation? Simply stated, the purpose of an investigation is to uncover the unknown information. On the other hand, the concept has a much broader application within an investigation. The unknown information may always remain unknown. In theory, there will always be a facet of information that remains unknown, and because of this, persistent unknown information can never be established with an absolute degree of certainty. However, through diagnostic methods and harnessing the known information, a reasonable degree of certainty can be established. The critical aspect of silent evidence is the application of hypothesis generation and testing. Through the use of hypotheses, alternative interpretations of information can be generated.

The issue of evidence perception is uniquely important to the criminal defense investigator. Not only is the criminal defense investigator required to set aside any personal bias and consistently check their own logic, but they must also address the possibility that available evidence can support more than one interpretation of an event. All possible interpretations, as well as the underlining quality of evidence supporting each possible interpretation, must be evaluated.

Chapter 4

Denial and Deception

Denial and deception should be at the forefront of a criminal defense investigator's thought process. Unfortunately, a wide array of reasons exist why information will be denied or the criminal defense investigator will be deceived. In short, denial and deception emerges from three main sources: the Defendant, witnesses, and law enforcement. The Criminal defense investigator must be cautious of this and consider the likelihood that denial and deception will occur.

Countering denial and deception is a critical task of the criminal defense investigator. Denial and deception are two of the three critical barriers to a successful criminal defense investigation. The third is the criminal defense investigator's own errors in critical thinking. The latter part of this book is devoted to the issue of critical thinking through the application of structured analysis techniques. To some degree, countering denial and deception is a collection issue; however, to a larger degree, it is an analytical issue. As a result, the issue is heavily tied to analytical judgments and the possibility of these judgements leading to catastrophic failure. This form of failure is driven by two components: information that is unknown to the criminal defense investigator because it has been "denied" and information that is manipulated to cause the criminal defense investigator to arrive at a false judgment due to intentional "deception."

The Defendant

The defendant, in many cases, is the primary source of denial and deception. The defendant may actively deceive by denying the criminal allegation lodged against them. This can occur through varying degrees of deception. The defendant may deceive the criminal defense investigator on critical aspects of the alleged crime. In other cases, the defendant may outwardly deny any involvement in the alleged crime. On the other hand, the defendant at times may withhold information that is critical to the criminal defense investigator's work. This form of denial will involves critical details of the incident. Any form of denial and deception on the part of the defendant can have a detrimental effect on the overall work product of the criminal defense investigator.

Denial and deception by the criminal defendant are critical issues for the criminal defense investigator. In general, two possible aspects will drive a defendant to employ denial or deception: embarrassment and manipulation.

The defendant may simply be embarrassed to admit their involvement in a criminal activity. This can emerge in varying degrees. The defendant may find a specific action undertaken during the alleged crime, or general involvement in a criminal activity, embarrassing. This embarrassment may come from the prospect of admitting involvement in the criminal activity to family and friends. More simply, the defendant may find embarrassment in admitting to the criminal activity in front of the criminal defense attorney. The defendant may feel the professionals working on his or her defense may become judgmental or reluctant to provide a vigorous defense.

More commonly, the defendant may be simply presenting manipulative behavior. Several hypotheses could be presented to argue the reasoning behind the manipulative behavior used by many criminal defendants. However, these hypotheses would have no utility. In reality, many criminal defendants are simply guilty of their accused crimes. Many criminal defendants live lifestyles based on criminal enterprises of thievery, illicit drug use, and general manipulative behavior. As a result, there is no reason, in the minds of the criminal defendant, to alter their behavior when represented by a criminal defense team. In turn, too many criminal defendants deny critical information or deceive the responsible criminal defense attorney and criminal defense investigator.

Unfortunately, any form of denial and deception employed by a criminal defendant only creates difficulties in their defense. The all-too-common occurrence of denial and deception causes many criminal defense attorneys and criminal defense investigators to form a bias regarding any information provided by criminal defendants. As a result, the criminal defense investigator must have considerable mental discipline in order to receive any defendant's statements at face value. However, the criminal defense investigator must at the same time determine the logical probability that the defendant's statements are true or deceptive. This is a critical aspect of handling and processing information received from a criminal defendant. The responsible criminal defense attorney has a considerable need to know if the defendant's version of events will ultimately withstand scrutiny during a criminal trial.

Witnesses

Witnesses to criminal activity present a unique set of problems for criminal defense investigators. This is especially true in the possibility of a witness engaging in any form of denial or deception. The reality is that most witnesses have very little vested interest in the defense of a criminal defendant.

Witness denial and deception should be expected and the utmost consideration should be given to this possibility when dealing with any witness, including any codefendants. Witnesses have considerable motivation not to become involved in any form of criminal proceedings. As a result, a witness may simply deny any knowledge of the alleged criminal activity. A witness may also employee deception. The motivations for this can vary widely. The witness may present an unknown bias in the form of a pre-conceived view of the defendant or may use their testimony as an opportunity for retribution for prior interactions with the defendant. In the most complex scenario, a witness may deploy deception in an attempt to hide their own involvement in the criminal activity or to protect a codefendant.

The most common and difficult issue in cases of witness denial and deception is the existence of a snitch or codefendant turned State witness. In both scenarios, a witness exists that has a vested interest in supporting the State's criminal hypotheses. Both types of witnesses receive some type of compensation for their testimony. In some cases, the witness may receive payment in monetary form. In other cases, the most common, they are receiving a reduction in sentencing or walking freely from an unrelated criminal charge. Nevertheless, the witness has ample reason to embellish or downright lie in their testimony.

A criminal defense investigator needs to be sensitive and highly detailed in determining and countering witness denial and deception. Every witness needs to be viewed as being highly likely to deny information or deceive the defense to some degree.

Law Enforcement

Law enforcement, including the prosecutor, uses denial and deception at a professional level. This denial and deception can be found from the initial criminal investigation through the criminal trial. In most cases, law enforcement will be observed simply denying information. Only in rare occasions will law enforcement employ true deception. Nevertheless, denial and deception on the part of law enforcement will be experienced in almost every single criminal defense investigation.

The foremost form of denial on the part of law enforcement will be found in official reporting. Any criminal defense investigator who practices in multiple jurisdictions will find that law enforcement reporting varies widely in style and content. Official reporting will be presented in a narrative format. These narratives will vary from the inclusion of low-level details to highly detailed reporting. The most common form of denial by law enforcement is the exclusion of information from official reporting. Unfortunately, law enforcement officers are extremely biased in their reporting. Law enforcement reporting, typically, only includes incriminating information. Any possible information suggesting innocence is simply omitted.

For example, it is all too common for a law enforcement officer to interview many witnesses but only document witness testimony that provides incriminating evidence. As a result, the witnesses who would create a reasonable doubt are left undocumented and unknown to the defense team and the court.

Law enforcement officers consistently omit any details that would allow an observer to gain an understanding of their tradecraft as investigators. This practice is based on a belief that if the general public had a detailed understanding of law enforcement tradecraft, criminals would only be more successful. However, this is a fallacy. The bulk of law enforcement tradecraft is clearly detailed in volumes of literature. Although law enforcement tradecraft is well documented in literature, the critical issue is whether specific law enforcement officers correctly utilize acceptable investigative methodologies. This becomes of critical importance when dealing with the collection of physical evidence, crime scene processing, and reconstructions. Without fully understanding how a specific law enforcement officer completed these tasks, there stands a chance that the law enforcement officer erroneously altered or failed to document physical evidence. In the case of a reconstruction, the law enforcement officer may reach a false analytical judgment.

The most extreme form of denial of information comes through failing to admitting to the existence of official documentation. This can be observed in many forms, but typically this form of denial is practiced by the prosecutor. In simple terms, the prosecutor has the overbearing intention to present the defendant as guilty. This is carried out by only presenting information demonstrating guilt and withholding any information proving or suggesting innocence. If the defense team is unaware of any official documentation that might suggest innocence, they are unable to cite it in discovery requests. Fortunately, this form of denial can be countered through analytical judgments.

Law enforcement deception is a critical concern for any practicing criminal defense investigator. Typically, the most common form of law enforcement deception is intentionally hiding information or omitting unintentional errors. This form of deception is the result of professional embarrassment, the drive to secure a conviction, or efforts to protect their career. Many individuals fail to remember that law enforcement officers are simply employees of their respective agencies. As a result, many forms of internal politics exist. These politics drive assignments and promotions. A law enforcement officer has more than ample motivation to hide their mistakes.

In extreme cases, law enforcement officers will commit acts of deception to secure a conviction. Many factors can drive this form of deception, including the factors mentioned above as well as political or personal bias. No matter the reasoning, intentional deception can be devastating to the defendant. These forms of deception can be observed in many forms, but the most common are false documentation, evidence tampering, and providing false testimony. Intentional deception is the worst case scenario and can reach a level of extreme complexity.

The criminal defense investigator must always consider the possibility of all varying forms of law enforcement denial and deception. There will always be some level of both throughout every criminal defense investigation, however, the key is determining the degree of denial and deception and whether it is acceptable. In many cases, the denial of information on the part of law enforcement is considered acceptable to some degree. In many cases, the courts and local laws support this behavior for varying reasons, based on politics and statutory law. Nevertheless, the criminal defense investigator needs to be sensitive to the possibility that these thresholds have been breached to the degree of unacceptability.

Chapter 5

The Theory of Criminal Defense Investigation

A criminal defense investigator spends their professional life immersed in issues of fact and fiction; without a framework, discerning between them can become a very abstract process. In simple terms, the criminal defense investigator's work includes sorting, measuring, and analyzing a huge amount of information. On a small scale this process can be overwhelming. Without a framework the practitioner is left to their own devices. The most usable framework is a working theory that remains flexible in its application from case to case.

Much like other private investigators, a criminal defense investigator is a broker of information. After all the hard work, critical thinking, and processing of information, the end result are simple written reports and a verbal briefing to the responsible criminal defense attorney. The critical concept in brokering information is knowing what is important and what is not. This can be difficult to discern for even the most experienced criminal defense investigator.

From the beginning of a criminal defense investigation, the responsible criminal defense attorney should be made aware of all information, with some exceptions. Any available information related to the defense of the accused should be made available. In terms of what should be included in written reports, non-critical tasks of making telephone calls to locate witnesses or trivial issues like which routes were driven during the investigation are of little value to the attorney. However, beyond this trivial information, every piece of information and its source should be made available to the criminal defense attorney. This includes both positive and negative information. Some investigators initially entering the criminal defense arena may balk at the idea of delivering information that may harm the defense to the responsible attorney, for example, information showing guilt. However, this type of information is by far as valuable as information showing innocence. When preparing for trial, the responsible criminal defense attorney must be aware of all available information in order to plan an intelligent argument. The criminal defense investigator should not make assumptions regarding what the criminal defense attorney may require. Needs will change during the lifespan of the defense, which may cause otherwise useless information to emerge as valuable.

The critical question is what type of information should be obtained. Without a proper collection theory or formal framework, figuring this out can be a very taxing process. Fortunately, a simple collection theory is adequate. This is a two-pronged approach comprised of a two-stage process. The first stage is the primary collection of information that is evidence of innocence. The second stage is the collection of information that discredits evidence of guilt. In simple terms, the primary goal is the collection of information proving the defendant's innocence. This collection theory is strictly followed and implemented through a wide array of methods.

In this book, collection theory refers to the process of collecting information. "Collection" is the process of collecting raw information that has not undergone some form of analysis. Although the term "collection" has not been traditionally used in the area of criminal investigation by practitioners in law enforcement or for-profit investigations, it is more definitive as to the stage of the investigation compared to the overall process of investigation.

In the two-pronged approach of collection, gathering evidence of innocence is the primary collection operation, done in order to discredit the State's criminal theory. In general, the State's criminal theory is not designed solely by the prosecutor as a rational independent actor. Instead, it is initially generated during law enforcement's criminal investigation. A brief review of law enforcement reporting will reveal the State's criminal theory with some marginal limitations, including the prosecutor's argumentative strategy when opposing the criminal defense attorney in court. These limitations to understanding the State's criminal theory are expected and can only be resolved as the criminal case progresses through the criminal justice system.

Beyond law enforcement reporting, the State's criminal theory will rest upon items of evidence, which are interpreted through the narrative constructed by law enforcement reporting and testimony in court. These items will range from written or recorded interviews to varying forms of evidence. In theory, all forms of evidence should be fully documented in law enforcement reporting. However, at times, because of errors, denial and deception, or bias recovered evidence will go undocumented in law enforcement reporting. The evidence may still be presented in the discovery file, or an indication of the evidence's existence may emerge through related evidence. For example, an audio recording made during a witness interview may contain the sound of a camera operation, but no photographs were provided by the State during discovery. A wide array of reasons can exist for this type of occurrence. Nevertheless, the criminal defense investigator's goal must be to obtain all evidence items in the State's possession. The key is knowing specifically *what* to request. This becomes especially important when the State is less than forthcoming. In practice, the criminal defense investigator will communicate the need for a discovery request to the responsible criminal defense attorney who will, in turn, engage the court.

The State's criminal theory will be driven by law enforcement and then augmented by the prosecutor. Bias is a significant aspect in law enforcement generating the initial raw criminal theory. During law enforcement's criminal investigation a considerable amount of evidence will be engaged and assessed, and then a limited amount of this evidence will be collected and documented in official law enforcement reporting. The problem with assessing evidence is that the process is based on perception, which is directly impacted by bias. As a result, during the law enforcement investigation, evidence that does not support the investigator's criminal theory is discounted as unrelated or simply ignored. Thus, important evidence, all too often, will not be collected and documented.

Uncollected and undocumented evidence is a critical issue for a criminal defense investigator. How does a criminal defense investigator uncover evidence that has been ignored by law enforcement? This process is comprised of reviewing the State's physical and testimonial evidence. Typically, physical evidence is simply reinterpreted and witness testimony recollected by the criminal defense investigator. Based upon the criminal defense investigator's interpretation of evidence and direct knowledge of witness testimony, an array of alternate criminal theories or an alternate evidence theory is generated, leading to a search for and collection of new or undocumented evidence. The initial primary goal should be the review of State evidence, followed by the uncovering of new or undisclosed evidence. At the onset of any criminal defense case, the primary analytical concern should be evidence of innocence in opposition to the State's evidence supporting the criminal case.

After reviewing and collecting new evidence, the second prong is used. The credibility of all known evidence is accessed, and discrediting information is collected. Based upon the author's professional experience, opinions differ on this aspect of a criminal defense investigation. In one view, the primary credibility concern should be that of the State's criminal theory, and all discrediting information should be collected. The opposing view is an approach that tests the credibility of all evidence, used both in the State's case and in the alternate evidence theory. The latter seems to be the most logical approach. When there is evidence proving guilt and an absence of evidence supporting innocence, the only option available is to discredit the evidence of guilt. On the other hand, evidence supporting an alternative criminal theory, which might include an alternative suspect, poses an additional risk. If this evidence is successfully challenged by the prosecutor than only the evidence brought forth by the State remains. Knowing the credibility of evidence supporting alternative theories is a matter of eliminating bias and possibly avoiding catastrophic failure in the defense of the accused.

The implementation of the two-pronged approach is not linear but an intertwined process of collection and analysis. This process produces a professional work product and is only successfully conducted by skilled practitioners. The criminal defense investigator is faced with many issues in the collection of information and the ensuing analysis. This book is not meant to address collection issues specifically. These issues are vast and vary from case to case. In reality, no written document could address the subject completely. In turn, practitioners rely on professional experience, local knowledge, and peer collaboration to address specific collection issues. However, specific issues in the area of analysis are within the reach of this book. Collection will be addressed but not on the level of "how" the information is collected; instead, this book considers collection needs driven by the demands of analysis.

Chapter 6

The Criminal Defense Investigation Cycle and Framework

The intertwined process of collection and analysis is dynamic. Traditional criminal investigation practices have been ill defined in academic literature and by criminal investigators. The subparts of the overall criminal investigation have been documented, from suspect interrogations to forensic practices. However, the overall process has been traditionally left to the practitioner's personal work habits, or at times, overly biased perceptions of reality. The overall investigative process is of key importance for the criminal investigator and the criminal defense investigator, in particular.

This book breaks from the traditional approach of presenting an undefined investigative process and adopts what is referred to as the analysis cycle, or specifically the Criminal Defense Investigative Cycle. In simple terms, the analysis cycle is the overall process that produces quality information for the consumption of the responsible criminal defense attorney. The purpose of the cycle is to assess and re-assess information in a loop over the lifespan of the investigation. In daily life, processes from business to personal tasks are linear in nature. A defined starting point exists with a defined conclusion. However, the Criminal Defense Investigative Cycle presented in this book is a closed loop with no predefined start or conclusion. In theory, the investigative process could progress into infinity without any real tangible conclusion and in some cases this will become reality.

In *Uncovering Reasonable Doubt: The Component Method,* Brandon Perron, a criminal defense investigator, presented a methodology for members of his profession.[12] This five-step process is essentially a high-level linear approach to completing criminal defense investigations:

1. Investigative Review of the discovery file, police reports; victim/witness statements, crime scene examinations, lab reports, etc.

2. Initial defendant interview

3. Crime scene examination, diagram, and photography

4. Victim/witness background investigation

5. Reporting of investigation and testifying[13]

Academically, the above five-step process includes well-defined high-level tasks. Perron's Component Method presents as a digestible and understandable process for a criminal defense investigator to utilize. The process does have undeniable utility and without doubt each "component" is a benchmark every criminal defense investigator must meet in professional practice. On the other hand, to a large degree, this methodology is presented as linear and is easily disrupted by outside demands and real world events and shifts: witnesses avoid interviews, crime scene access is withheld, or the scene has been distorted by events following the original incident. A criminal defense investigator is not only faced with field operational issues but also with the tactics utilized by opposing attorneys. The reality is that discovery materials arrive late and at times are withheld into the lifespan of an investigation. These two factors coupled will disrupt any linear investigation more times than not. Without a considerable amount of experience and skill, any criminal defense investigator can become misguided. In turn, a flexible robust framework is required.

Intelligence practitioners utilize a process that is referred to as the "intelligence cycle." This cycle is a high-level closed-loop process. In simple terms, information is collected and processed, intelligence is produced and communicated to the consumer, and new needs are

---

[12] Perron, Brandon A. Uncovering Reasonable Doubt, 1998.

[13] Ibid., p. 1-5

communicated followed by the process looping over and over. Figure 7.1 represents the intelligence cycle.

A criminal defense investigator works in an environment that is different to some extent than that in which intelligence practitioners operate. Both practitioners face issues ranging from collection, accessing needs, and the processing of information. However, criminal defense investigators differ from intelligence practitioners in their provision of information to a different consumer.

Intelligence practitioners must provide and communicate information, known as intelligence, to a wide array of individuals across all levels of a governmental structure. These individuals range from low-level operational personal to the highest level of decision making authority. These individuals are considered "consumers."[14] Consumers utilize the communicated intelligence to make decisions at their level of authority. As a result, the intelligence is utilized based upon the consumer's authority level.

The consumer receives information labeled as "intelligence." This is an important distinction. "Intelligence" is distinct from raw information. In short, raw information from collection efforts is driven through the intelligence cycle. Specifically, the raw information must undergo analysis by an intelligence analyst before it is labeled as "intelligence." This distinction drives the reporting a consumer receives. Depending on the consumer's level of authority, little to no background is provided in the form of raw information. The reporting, considered an intelligence product, will often simply be the intelligence analyst's assessment of the specific information. Information provided by a criminal defense investigator to a consumer, the responsible attorney, differs greatly from these intelligence products.

---

[14] In the context of this book, the term "consumer" refers to the individual who utilizes the information provided by the criminal defense investigator. In general, this individual is primarily the responsible Criminal Defense Attorney. However, in the case of a criminal trial, the court is also the Consumer.

Figure 7.1 - Intelligence Cycle

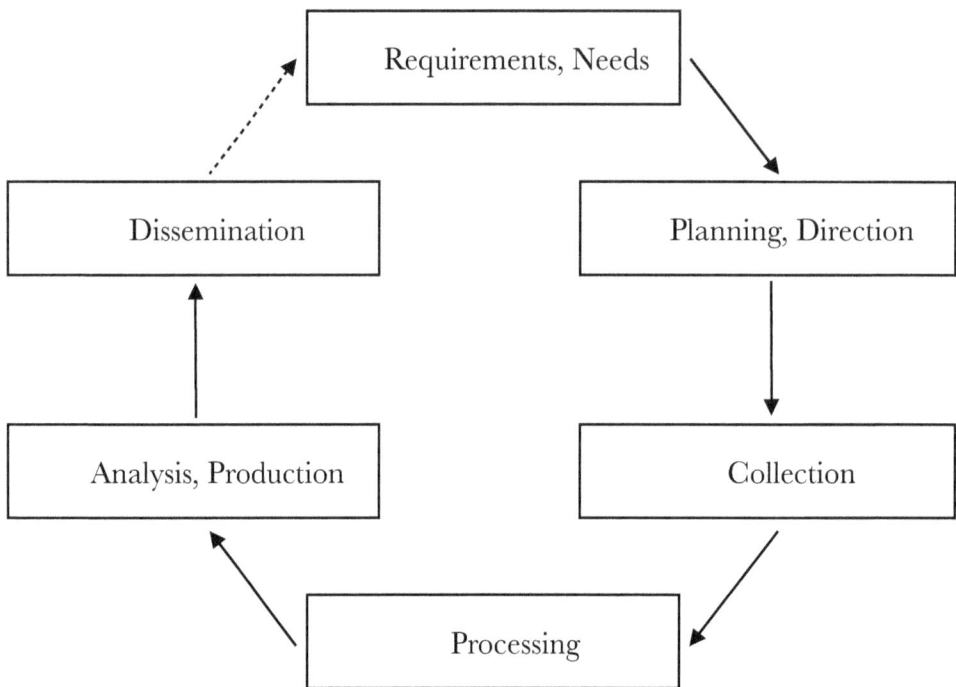

A criminal defense investigator's reporting is much broader and has to meet a wider demand. In one respect, the practitioner has to communicate an expert opinion in the same way as an intelligence analyst does. However, the criminal defense investigator must also meet the demands of the criminal defense attorney, which differ greatly from those of a typical government decision maker.

Attorneys are unique consumers. All raw information must be accessible to the criminal defense attorney in the greatest detail. For example, reporting on a witness interview must have detailed information on the witness testimony. Essentially, the attorney must obtain a detailed understanding of the interview, which typically is only gained from being involved in the interview directly. This level of detail and accuracy must be consistent across all reporting produced by the criminal defense investigator.

Beyond the raw details of investigative operations, the criminal defense investigator must also communicate an expert opinion. This expert opinion is objective logical reasoning gained through investigative methodologies and the application of structured analysis. In short, the criminal defense investigator's expert opinion is the final result of the analysis cycle.

The responsible attorney essentially represents a second analytical layer but presents a different perspective. The criminal defense investigator's domain is objective logical reasoning. This perspective is grounded in the objective assessment of evidence leading to a logical conclusion. On the other hand, the attorney's perspective is grounded in the interpretation of law and skilled arguments in relation to presented evidence. In simple terms, the criminal defense investigator is responsible for producing an objective investigative product, and the attorney is responsible for exploiting the investigative product. The work process shared by the criminal defense investigator and criminal defense attorney drives the analysis cycle.

The Criminal Defense Investigation Cycle

Much like the intelligence cycle used by intelligence practitioners, a criminal defense investigator can apply a specific intelligence cycle to a criminal defense investigation. This is referred to as the Criminal Defense Investigation Cycle. This process is specific to the information and issues encountered by criminal defense investigators. Using a specific structured cycle during an investigation holds many benefits. This process gives the investigation articulable structure, clarity, and, most importantly, actionable utility.

The term "actionable utility" refers to a functional use—utility—and information that can be acted upon—which is actionable. This is two-part concept. A method or concept may have utility but lack any actionable results. For example, a criminal defense investigator may have access to aerial imagery of an alleged crime scene covering two square miles. In theory, this imagery would hold considerable utility. However, when visiting the location and making a physical assessment of the area, the Investigator is faced with the fact that this location has been completely changed by urban development, which occurred after the alleged incident. As a result, the aerial imagery may seem to have utility, considering the many possible uses for the data it includes. However, the imagery presents no actionable utility because the interim changes in the landscape mean that the data cannot be confirmed or acted upon in the present.

The Criminal Defense Investigation Cycle is meant to act as a framework. A criminal defense investigator works in an extremely abstract environment. In many cases, this environment is not easily understood by the criminal defense investigator. Defining investigative goals, collection needs, and analysis needs present varying challenges from case to case. However, the theoretical lens used by a criminal defense investigator to view and access the investigative landscape should be founded in the Criminal Defense Investigative Cycle, which consists of the following five-step process:

1. Defining the issue
2. Collection
3. Model construction
4. All source analysis
5. Diagnostic analysis
6. Retracing

The Criminal Defense Investigation Cycle is a closed-loop process with a redundant feedback loop. Figure 7.2 illustrates this cycle. In theory, there is no predefined starting point in the Criminal Defense Investigation Cycle. However, in practice, this process will more than likely start at the stage of receiving information, which is typically at the point when the criminal defense investigator's services are retained by an attorney and the issue of the investigation is defined. Initially the criminal defense investigator will receive information from the attorney in the form of a discovery file. This may include a limited amount of information initially and then grow in volume as the discovery process unfolds between the defense attorney and the State. Nevertheless, this information is almost always the starting point of a criminal defense investigation.

70

Figure 7.2 - Criminal Defense Investigation Cycle

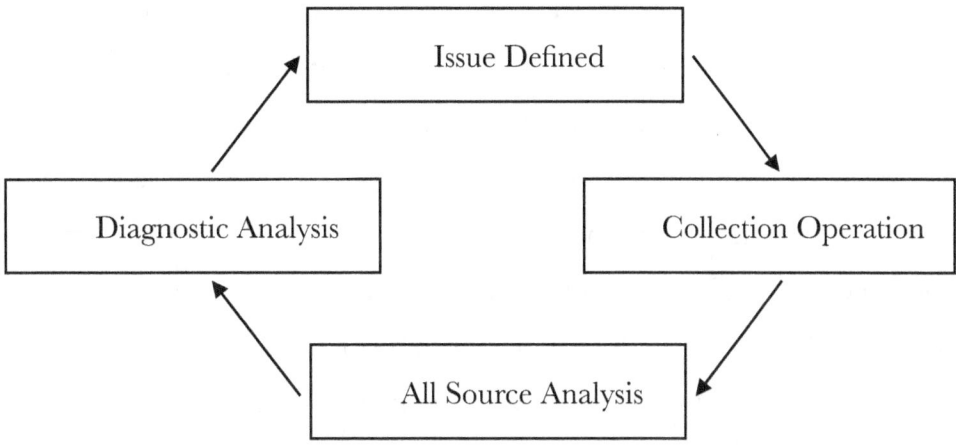

Understanding the overall process of the Criminal Defense Investigation Cycle is important and required for successful completion. Arguably, this process could be depicted as linear with a defined starting and ending point. However, a linear approach would create information processing errors. This type of error is due to unrecognized or unavailable information at varying points throughout the life the investigation. Thus, a "looping action" is used to process and then reprocess information as new information emerges and needs change within the investigation.

Defining the issues is the first step initiated by the criminal defense investigator and is a task repeated throughout the lifespan of an investigation. This stage of the Criminal Defense Investigation Cycle is by far the most difficult and, if not properly implemented, can cause catastrophic failure. In simple terms, this stage is the process of defining the issue faced by the criminal defense investigator. For example, what specific investigative issues exist within the alleged crime? At a strategic level, the issue is the criminal allegation lodged against the defendant. However, defining the issue is much more complex, and a simplistic approach is neither desirable nor productive. In reality, the criminal defense investigator is faced with defining not one issue, but an array of issues. Issue definition is the foundation of the Criminal Defense Investigation Cycle.

Collection is the typical task envisioned by most consumers of information who retain the services of a criminal defense investigator. However, this is only one facet of the criminal defense investigator's overall work product. Collection operations entail a wide array of tasks. Interviewing witnesses, documenting a scene, and collecting physical evidence falls into this category. Unfortunately, collection has become the main focus of the State's criminal investigators and the opposing criminal defense investigators. Typically, a collection operation is the initial stage of a criminal investigation or criminal defense investigation and is followed by a sparing level of analysis, which is slanted more towards legal analysis than any real analysis of the alleged crime. In terms of the Criminal Defense Investigative Cycle, collection is the second stage of the overall loop and feedback cycle.

During the onset of a criminal defense investigation, the first collection operation will be receiving the discovery file from the responsible attorney. This form of collection will reoccur in large complex defense cases as the case matures overtime. Secondly, collection operations will occur as investigative needs are identified. The process of interviewing witnesses, collecting physical evidence, documenting alleged crime scenes, and many other collection tasks that will emerge as a need throughout the lifespan of the case. This information, in all cases of criminal defense, fall into the categories of temporal, geospatial, topical, and network data. The key principle in discriminating between a collection task and an analytical task is that collection is the process of collecting or receiving information from a person, location, or some form of digital repository. You simply obtain the information. The interpretation of the information is generated through analysis. Following a collection operation, the new information is organized across a model.

Model construction is another foundation point in the Criminal Defense Investigation Cycle and is the cycle's third stage. In general, after receiving the initial information (discovery file) and all information generated through filed collection operations, the information is assessed through the General Criminal Defense Investigative Model. The model is used to give the information structure and actionable utility. Using the model, the criminal defense investigator is able to identify gaps that exist within the information. The initial information will provide real data structure to the General Criminal Defense Investigative Model. However, there will still be a considerable amount of absent model structure after accessing the initial information received at the onset of the case. The areas of absent structure within the General Criminal Defense Investigative Model are information gaps and require collection operations to eliminate them. As the loop and feedback cycle occurs, these information gaps will be reduced in size and frequency through repeated collection operations. Over the lifespan of the investigation, the model's information needs should be completely fulfilled, unless uncontrollable circumstances exist.

The construction of the General Criminal Defense Investigative Model is not a collection operation or a task rooted in analysis. However, there is considerable overlap in the practice of collection and analysis. A model is the breaking point between collection and analysis. New information is generated and organized across the structure of the model and then exploited through analysis. For example, if a phonebook consisted of a list of random telephone numbers without any form of organization, it would present no real utility and would be nothing more than a box of paper with random numbers on each page. In simple terms, a model represents information obtained through collection operations in an organized structure that enables analysis. The model's validity is measured by the quality of information catalogued within the model.

All source analysis is the accumulation and combining of the information described above through collection and modeling. In general, following the collection operation, the General Criminal Defense Investigative Model should be a coherent dataset, which represents a prior event in history, the alleged crime. The model is then exploited through structured analysis. The combination of these analytical techniques represents the all source analysis, which is specific to the criminal defense investigator's work product.

Diagnostic analysis is the true exploitation of the General Criminal Defense Investigative Model coupled with all source analysis. If the Criminal Defense Investigation Cycle was a linear process, diagnostic analysis would be the final step. However, this is not the case. The Criminal Defense Investigation Cycle is meant to exploit information to the furthest degree possible. As a result, the work product produced during all source analysis is further refined through diagnostic analysis methodologies. In simple terms, this stage in the Criminal Defense Investigation Cycle is where the General Criminal Defense Investigative Model's structure is tested using an array of hypotheses. One structured analysis method is known as the "analysis of competing hypotheses."

The diagnostic analysis step of the Criminal Defense Investigation Cycle represents a critical stage in the lifecycle of any criminal defense investigation. However, this stage should be experienced more than once in any investigation. Three critical goals are met through diagnostic analysis: diagnostic testing of the State's criminal theory, generation of alternate defense theories, and the identification of additional collection needs. As a result, the criminal defense investigation is able to gain a robust focus by absolutely refuting the State's criminal theory, identifying weaknesses in the State's criminal theory, and providing alternate criminal theories, which can be exploited by the criminal defense investigator through further investigation and analysis. Moreover, the responsible defense attorney is able to exploit this same information in court.

Following the completion of diagnostic analysis two events will occur. In most cases, diagnostic analysis will identify a need for further collection. This collection may be driven by the generation of alternate criminal theories or identified information gaps, which have hindered diagnostic analysis. Second, it is very likely that the State will submit additional information, which is intended to be used at trial by the State. In either case, the criminal defense investigator is faced with new information to collect and assess. As a result, the Criminal Defense Investigation Cycle starts over once again. This is known as the feedback loop or retrace. Any time new information is received or the need for collection is identified, the Criminal Defense Investigation Cycle is restarted. Regardless of the reason for new collection and analysis, the process is initiated at the issue defining stage. In practice, the Criminal Defense Investigation Cycle will be a repeating process of receiving or uncovering new information, adding the information to the General Criminal Defense Investigative Model, generating all source analysis, and completing a diagnostic analysis.

As an academic exercise, the Criminal Defense Investigative Cycle is a straightforward process of repeating stages as new information emerges. In practice, the application of the cycle is less than ideal and can be chaotic at times. A criminal defense investigator can become easily taxed by the sheer volume of information to process. This is of special concern. If the Criminal Defense Investigative Cycle is viewed as an assembly line of gathering and processing information, the process will fail. The key question is when to stop collection operations and exploit the information through analysis. There is no simple answer to this question. Many variables come into play. There is an extreme temptation to identify what information is needed, collect the information, and then process it through analysis, only repeating this process with minimum frequency.

In the ideal situation, the Criminal Defense Investigative Cycle is utilized through the concept of "small batches." The most extreme example of this is when each new segment of information is processed through the Criminal Defense Investigative Cycle. For example, one witness is identified and interviewed, the resulting information is organized across the General Criminal Defense Investigative Model, the all source analysis is completed, and then diagnostic analysis is completed. The loop is then completed by defining the next issue, and the same process is followed. This process of looping would be repeated for each witness, physical evidence, or any other form of information collected. On the other hand, a "big batch" concept, the opposing extreme, would entail only completing the loop twice: once during the onset of the investigation and then a second time during a sweep to close information gaps. In practice, this would be observed with additional loops as new information arrived through the discovery process, but the core investigation would only entail two passes through the Criminal Defense Investigative Cycle. For practicing criminal defense investigators, the Criminal Defense Investigative Cycle should be utilized on the smallest batch scale, when feasible in the face of operational issues. From day to day, a criminal defense investigator has to balance three distinctive issues. First is the issue of field collection operations. Second is the processing (or analysis) of information derived from field collection operations. Third is the issue of scheduling concurrent case work. The temptation to utilize the Criminal Defense Investigative Cycle as an assembly line to complete an investigation is rooted in these issues and from an inadequate understanding of the utility of structured analysis. The criminal defense investigator must exercise discipline in applying the Criminal Defense Investigative Cycle by ensuring information is collected and processed in the smallest batch possible. The only real driver that should be allowed to disrupt the concept of small batch processing should by the uncontrollable availability and cooperation of witnesses. However, a skilled criminal defense investigator should be able overcome most reasonable issues faced in this area of collection through experience, proper planning, and the application of collection tradecraft. The criminal defense investigator needs to maintain extreme discipline in applying small batch processing, to the degree of rejecting a proposed criminal defense investigation that would exhaust available investigative manpower resources.

Reporting Investigative Information

One critical aspect of the Criminal Defense Investigation Cycle that has been omitted until this point is the issue of reporting. This omission has been made to allow a clear review of the issue of analysis. Communicating the findings of a criminal defense investigation is critical to the overall success of the investigation endeavor. No matter how well a criminal defense investigation is completed, absolute failure will be experienced if the investigative findings are inadequately communicated to the responsible criminal defense attorney.

Two main issues exist within the communication of investigative results. First, the criminal defense investigator will produce raw investigative information during collection efforts, resulting from a wide array of investigative tasks, from witness interviews to documenting alleged crime scenes. Second, the criminal defense investigator will produce analytical products, which are the direct result of structured analysis. These two different investigative actions must both be clearly communicated to the responsible attorney. However, the end results of both investigative actions are starkly different. Both are evidence and could be used in a criminal proceeding. Raw investigative data needs to be communicated without any interpretation. There are borderline exceptions to this rule that rest on the criminal defense investigator's need to descriptively articulate observations and capture an adequate account of events. Nevertheless, the criminal defense investigator should avoid an interpretation of raw investigative information in the original source reporting. On the other hand, when communicating analytical products, also known as the investigator's expert opinion, the criminal defense investigator is communicating an interpretation of raw investigative information. These different types of information (with and without interpretation) require two different reporting methods for raw information and analytical products.

When preparing reports in general, several common formatting styles should be avoided. Avoid the use of bullets; these should only be used in rare circumstances when reporting information that would confuse the reader in paragraph form. Bullets should not be used as a crutch for weak writing skills. Reporting should be clear and concise. The reader should not be left confused or questioning any statement made by a witness due to ambiguous reporting. A criminal defense investigator should take considerable care to not alter the narrative of the subject action detailed in any reporting. All reporting should fully describe the subject action in considerable detail. A criminal defense investigator should err of the side of caution by not reducing the complex process of any investigative action into a short report on the basis of laziness and or the inability to communicate effectively in writing. For every thirty minutes spent in field collection or analysis, the criminal defense investigator should invest at least two hours in report preparation. Although this ratio will vary depending on the experience and skill of the criminal defense investigator in preparing reports, this ratio should be used as a benchmark for time management.

The two methods of reporting are provided to the responsible criminal defense attorney at two different stages of the Criminal Defense Investigation Cycle. Figure 7.3 illustrates the different stages of reporting non-interpreted and interpreted information to the responsible attorney. The reporting of information that is not interpreted is delivered during the collection of raw investigative information, while the reporting containing the investigator's interpretation of information is released during the all source and diagnostic analysis stages.

Figure 7.3 - Criminal Defense Investigation Cycle Reporting

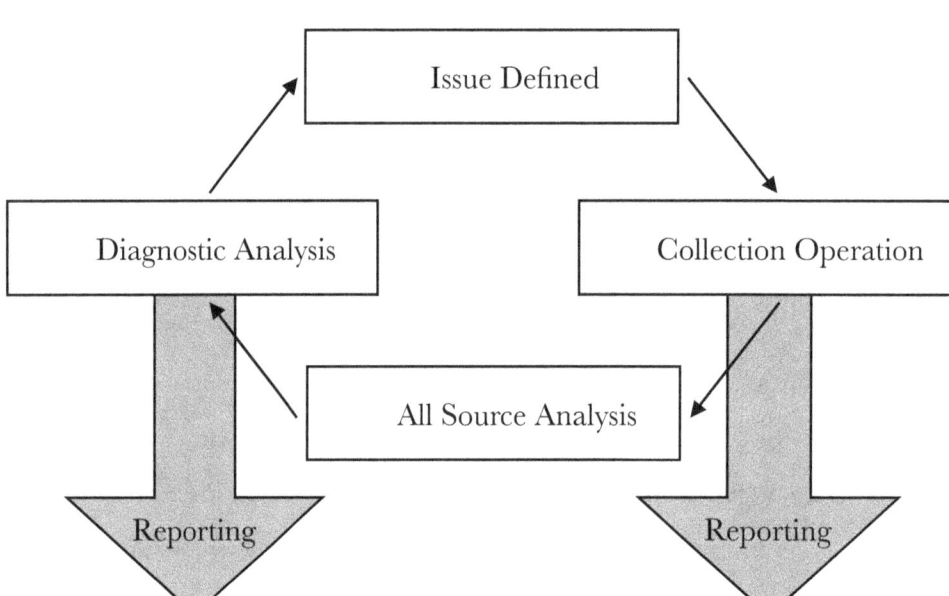

All raw investigative information is reported through a written narrative titled "Memorandum of Investigation." A Memorandum of Investigation is utilized in real time during collection efforts. For example, when a witness is interviewed, a Memorandum of Investigation is produced to clearly communicate the information uncovered during the interview to the responsible Attorney. A Memorandum of Investigation is a highly detailed written narrative. The goal is to provide a level of detail that could only be experienced by

78

an individual personally observing the event. This is a high benchmark for the criminal defense investigator to achieve. In reality, no matter how skilled the criminal defense investigator is as a writer, this level will remain elusive. Nevertheless, this theoretical benchmark illustrates the critical need to provide detailed and accurate reporting to the responsible attorney.

A three-part Memorandum of Investigation is utilized. Typically written on letterhead, the Memorandum of Investigation presents the initial text, which is essentially an introduction. This paragraph is generic in nature and identifies the following information:

- Date and time of action
- Location of action
- How the event occurred
- Reason for action
- Who was involved
- That the party involved was advised of who the criminal defense investigator represents and in what criminal proceeding

The introductory paragraph is followed by the body of the Memorandum of Investigation. The content in this section of the report will vary greatly. Some reports will have a body made up of only a couple of lines, while others will consist of several pages of text. The content within the body of the Memorandum of Investigation will be specific to the subject of the report, which may be a witness interview, physical evidence collection, or any other number of investigative collection tasks. The only real requirements of the body, beyond the detail already discussed, are the following elements:

- Chronological order of events
- Use of direct quotes from witnesses and not misdirecting the context from which the statement was made
- If a process is described, describe the process in a degree of detail that would allow the same process to be repeated by a third party

The closing text of the Memorandum of Investigation follows the body. This closing text may be presented in more than one paragraph, but typically one paragraph will be sufficient. This closing text is meant to advise the reader of any information that was not appropriate to or would break the chronological order of the Memorandum of Investigation's body text. The following information is typically presented in the closing text:

- Physical description of witnesses
- Criminal defense investigator's impressions of credibility in speech and physical demeanor specific to witnesses
- Reason why specific information was unobtainable
- Collection of any evidence and through what means
- Disposal of any evidence collected

All analytical products, the results produce through analysis, are reported through a written narrative titled "Memorandum." A Memorandum can be presented in many forms depending on the analytical product. These analytical products cover a wide area of topics from the criminal defense investigator's opinion to the results of the application of structured analysis. The possibilities are too vast to adequately describe how a Memorandum should be written. However, the following guidelines should be adhered to while preparing these documents:

- Do not use ambiguous language
- Clearly separate known information from analytical judgments
- Clearly identify the source of information discussed or analyzed throughout the report
- If a process is described, describe the process in a degree of detail that would allow the same process to be repeated by a third party

Preparing written reports is one of the most critical tasks performed by a criminal defense investigator. All reporting most be clear, concise, and demonstrate a consistent reporting and formatting style.

Chapter 7

All Source Analysis

Criminal defense investigations require a robust information flow. This information must be directly and coherently communicated to the responsible defense attorney. The mistake made by many professional investigators attempting to enter the arena of criminal defense investigation is the misconception that there is a complete focus on collection. All too often, they perceive this profession as one consisting only of interviewing witness, documenting the alleged crime scene, and completing background checks on individuals named as witnesses for the State. However, a complete criminal defense investigation includes much more than just collecting information. Moreover, the process does not include limited analysis of one segment of the alleged incident. The goal is to provide the responsible criminal defense attorney with a clear image of the entire alleged event.

A clear image of the alleged event is provided through all source analysis. In simple terms, all facets of the alleged incident are accessed and examined in detail. This process is the accumulation of the State's evidence and evidence uncovered by the criminal defense investigator, which is then driven through a comprehensive analysis process. Information used in this process can arrive in a wide array of forms.

The most common forms of evidence include:

- Witness testimony

- Expert testimony

- Law enforcement testimony

- Physical items (large items to trace evidence)

- Official reports

- Official records

- Third party records

- Photographs

- Video footage

- Evidence internally generated by the criminal defense investigator

Each type of information has a unique aspect in analysis. The process used to handle witness testimony will differ from the handling of physical evidence. However, all forms of information must be incorporated during the final analysis to generate a cohesive image of the alleged incident.

During criminal defense investigations, all source analysis includes the accumulation of witness testimony, evidence in the form of physical items or specimens, documents, records, and accepted scientific knowledge. "All source analysis" is a term meant to convey the process of analyzing all facets of an issue; it is not meant to represent a specific method of structured analysis.

Any all source analysis should include the following four categories of data, which make up any event in history, and are of special interest to the criminal defense investigator:

- Temporal (Time)
- Geospatial (Location)
- Topical (Content)
- Network (Relationships)

The temporal category views an event based upon time. When did an event start? When did the event end? What relationship or impact does one event have on another based upon the time at which the two events occurred? These types of questions are the foundation of assessing an overall event from a temporal perspective. The event is assessed through deconstruction and assessing each segment of the event based upon their chronological order. In simple terms, each segment of the event is assessed based upon time, specifically how the segment is connected to the proceeding segment, which provides a detailed examination of the overall event from a temporal view.

Geospatial data refers to information regarding the event's location or locations. Where did the event occur? Is there more than one location to consider? How are differing locations connected? These types of questions form the foundation for assessing an event from a geospatial perspective. As in a temporal analysis, geospatial information is deconstructed and assessed based upon the location characteristics and how it is connected to other locations of interest.

Topical data is information related to the event's content. Simply stated, a topical view of an event is the event's narrative. Generally, during a criminal investigation a narrative of the event is established through witness testimony, which is a simplistic approach. However, from the perspective of a criminal defense investigation, the event's narrative is represented not only through witness testimony but through all raw information not represented in a temporal, geospatial, or network form. In any criminal defense investigation, there is a considerable volume of topical information. In short, topical information is represented by all testimony, physical, and analytical evidence. Combined, this evidence represents the event's narrative or content.

Network data pertains to information regarding the event's internal and external relationships. In a criminal defense investigation, a network surpasses the limitations of a peer-to-peer network and incorporates not only individual associations and relationships but also their connection to locations, physical items or trace evidence, time, and the subject event from an external view.

Structured Analysis

In the following chapters, considerable attention is paid to the application of structured analysis methods. All source analysis constitutes the combined application of these methods. Each criminal defense investigation is unique, and at times one or more of the following methods may be used. In some cases, a method may not be need. However, the available information within each case will drive which methods are utilized.

The term "structured analysis" is used throughout this book, and it is the foundation of the theory and methods presented. Defining structured analysis can be a complex task, considering there are hundreds of methods employed and new methods are regularly developed to meet new needs. However, in *Structured Analytic Techniques for Intelligence Analysis*, Richard Heure and Randolph Pherson developed a taxonomy for structured analysis techniques. An examination of this taxonomy enables the reader to gain an understanding of how structured analysis compares to traditional approaches of assessing information.

In Heure and Pherson's taxonomy, two systems of thinking are presented: System 1 Thinking and System 2 Thinking. System 1 Thinking involves the traditional approach to intelligence analysis using intuitive judgement. Investigators, criminal investigators, and criminal defense investigators have traditionally utilized System 1 Thinking. In general, System 1 Thinking is an approach based upon subject-matter expertise coupled with basic cognitive skills.[15] In contrast, System 2 Thinking is based upon four categories: critical thinking, structured analysis, quasi-quantitative analysis, and empirical analysis.[16] The theory and methods presented in this book pertain to the areas of critical thinking and structured analysis.

---

[15] Richards, H J, and R H Pherson. Structured Analytic Techniques for Intelligence Analysis. 2nd ed. Thousand Oaks: CQ Press, 2015., p. 19

[16] Ibid., p. 22-23

Critical thinking, in Heure and Pherson's taxonomy, is the "application of the process and values of scientific inquiry" to the matter under investigation.[17] A critical thinker understands the need to check key assumptions, access contradictory information, and assess an array of possibilities.[18]

Structured analysis is conducted through a step-by-step process unitized by the investigator that externalizes the investigator's thinking. This process makes the investigator's thought process and logical reasoning "readily apparent to others, thereby enabling it to be reviewed, discussed, and critiqued."[19]

Structured analysis techniques are organized into eight families:

1. Decomposition and visualization

2. Idea generation

3. Scenarios and indicators

4. Hypothesis generation and testing

5. Assessment of cause and effect

6. Challenge analysis

7. Conflict management

8. Decision support[20]

Each family includes a wide array of structured analysis techniques. In general, the broad spectrum of these eight families is beyond the scope of this book. However, a discussion of structured analysis techniques belonging to the families of decomposition and visualization, idea generation, hypothesis generation and testing, and assessment of cause and effect is included. Not all the techniques in these four families are discussed, but a select group that have been found particularly effective in criminal defense by this author. Many

---

[17] Ibid., p. 22

[18] Ibid.

[19] Ibid., p.23

[20] Ibid., p. 25

additional techniques exist and are available for use in criminal defense. This book is by no means meant to suggest the techniques contained within this book are the only ones available and appropriate.

The application of structured analysis holds two important aspects for the criminal defense investigator. The first is the ability to process information in a predefined organized manner. This is a complex task, considering at times the criminal defense investigator will be required to process and gain an understanding of an overwhelming amount of information. However, this understanding is not just how the crime allegedly occurred, but what each specific segment of information represents across the event in question? Structured analysis gives the criminal defense investigator a framework from which to gain this footing and communicate this understanding clearly.

The second aspect is the diagnostic capability achieved through the application of structured analysis. In simple terms, structured analysis is formalized critical thinking; it is guided by a framework of predefined steps. The investigator is not limited by this framework but rather utilizes the framework as a roadmap insuring the complete terrain has been traveled. Some structured analytical techniques are specific to particular areas of concern. For example, hypothesis generation techniques are meant to generate hypotheses and not analyzing events over a period of time. On the other hand, some techniques are applicable very broadly. For example, the technique known as "analysis of competing hypotheses" has been utilized in a wide array of applications and diverse lines of inquiry. Regardless of the technique, all structured analytical techniques hold some degree of diagnostic capability.

In simple terms, information is organized, allowing knowledge extraction to occur. Some intelligence analysts, the traditional practitioners of structured analysis, group structured analysis techniques as either "diagnostic" or "non-diagnostic." This is understandable from the intended use of the specific structured analytical technique. For example, hypothesis generation techniques have traditionally not been considered diagnostic techniques. On the other hand, the technique of analysis of competing hypotheses has been considered the most robust diagnostic method developed to date. However, both, hypothesis generation techniques and analysis of competing hypotheses perform the key task of discriminating between options. Thus, a diagnostic decision is made through their application.

Through the use of structured analysis, a criminal defense investigator is able to process, organize, and make diagnostic judgements. However, this highlights an important aspect when considering the issue of diagnostic judgements. Is the work product generated through structured analysis evidence or simply an investigative aid? In some cases, the end work product, in whole or in part, can be used as evidence. In most cases, the work product will be utilized in part. For example, a diagram illustrating a peer-to-peer network will be used instead of the complete analysis process that generated the diagram, which could constitute hundreds of documents. Thus, the end work product of the specific structured analysis technique is utilized as evidence instead of the complete analytical process.

Structured analysis, by its very nature, is an investigative aid. First, the in-depth process of using a step-by-step technique allows the investigator to organize and sort through information. In turn, the diagnostic benefits found in this process act as robust instruments of inquiry. Second, the end result of each specific structured technique can be passed through an additional technique for further refinement. Not only does structured analysis act as an investigative aid, but the end work product can be utilized in the future as an instrument of inquiry or evidence.

Part 2

Chapter 8

Defining the Issue

Doing any type of investigation, the first goal must be defining the focus and breadth of the investigation. A criminal defense investigation is no different, and in this type of investigation, defining the fundamental issue or issues is undertaken both at the onset of the investigation and throughout the entire lifespan of the investigation.

Initial Criminal Defense Investigation Checklist

The onset of a criminal defense investigation can be overwhelming. For a novice perspective, an investigation may seem to be a straightforward process: the defendant is accused of a crime, the criminal defense investigator completes tasks A through Z, and the results are communicated to the responsible attorney. However, in reality, this the process is not that simple. Each defense investigation is unique and has special issues and needs that the criminal defense investigator must resolve and meet.

The initial stage of a criminal defense investigation is critical. Many investigations will require an A through Z approach. However, many others will result in a somewhat limited approach. In simple terms, the criminal defense investigator will be required to resolve only a specific issue. For example, some investigations will only consist of interviewing a witness, while others will entail a large, complex set of investigative operations. The key is to determine the specific needs of the investigation before any investigative task is undertaken. After determining the specific needs, a specific investigative strategy can be developed.

Typically, a criminal defense investigation will be prompted and initiated by the responsible criminal defense attorney by retaining the services of the criminal defense investigator. However, in some cases, the defendant or the defendant's family will retain the criminal defense investigator' services. In the author's experience, requests for an investigation at the initial trial level are typically prompted by the responsible attorney, and most post-trial criminal defense investigations are prompted by the defendant. As a result, the initial intake process of a new criminal defense investigation can vary widely depending on who has prompted the investigation. Thus, the investigator needs an efficient means of meeting these requests that will enable a successful resolution.

The criminal defense investigator has an absolute need for an efficient and diagnostic approach when accepting new cases. This is not a matter of communication, business process, or legal agreement, but one of determining the specific needs of each case. The criminal defense investigator should utilize a structured checklist as part of the initial intake process when accepting a new case.

The checklist should include the following questions, which should be addressed explicitly by the criminal defense investigator:

1. What criminal allegation prompted the need for a criminal defense investigation?

2. Is the criminal defense investigator appropriately licensed to investigate the allegation? Is there a possibility that the investigation will require additional licensing?

3. What are the key defense questions that needs to be answered?

4. How can a criminal defense investigation make a unique and meaningful contribution?

5. Have the key defense questions or similar questions already been answered by the criminal defense investigator or law enforcement?

6. Who are the principle consumers of the criminal defense investigation? Will their needs be addressed through the criminal defense investigation?

7. What are the possible answers to the key defense questions? What alternative explanations should be considered before making a determination?

8. Would the criminal defense investigation benefit from structured analysis techniques?

9. What potential sources of information would be beneficial in answering the defense's questions? Are the sources available?

10. Where should the criminal defense investigator seek assistance, information, or expertise during the investigation?

11. Should a brainstorming session be utilized to identify key assumptions, alternative criminal theories, or potential drivers of the criminal allegation?

12. What is the best way to communicate the results of the investigation? Should parts of the results be represented through diagrams or charts?[21]

The Initial Criminal Defense Investigation Checklist is a structured analysis technique. Each question should be independently, critically accessed before an investigation is initiated. In turn, key points are accessed. For example, the checklist forces the criminal defense investigator to assess possible source of information. In the case of a crime that allegedly occurred twenty years prior, information sources will be a significant issue. The investigator will have to critically assess the availability of information and may even reject the case on this basis, depending on the needs of the investigation. Thus, the Initial Criminal Defense Investigation Checklist is a critical assessment of the proposed investigation and the likely issues that the criminal defense investigator will face if they choose to proceed.

The initial stages of a criminal defense investigation are largely a routine process. The same type of information is requested from the criminal defense attorney in all cases. This information could be viewed as foundation information. Without this information, no real actionable utility can be realized. However, the criminal defense investigator must realize this

_____

[21]Adapted from: Richards, H J, and R H Pherson. Structured Analytic Techniques for Intelligence Analysis. 2nd ed. Thousand Oaks: CQ Press, 2015., p 48

is only a starting point and the ensuing search for information is never routine. Once the foundation information is received, the actual investigation begins.

During any criminal defense investigation the following information should be collected.

1. All law enforcement reporting

2. All known witnesses' information

3. All witness statements

4. All photographs, video footage, and diagrams

5. All lab reporting

6. All evidence handling documentation

7. Information identifying all involved law enforcement officers and support personnel

8. Law enforcement and support personnel training and personnel records, including CVs

9. Appropriate law enforcement agency policy and procedures

10. Any reporting prepared by a non-law enforcement agency and information on involved personnel

As a matter of course, most of the above information should be contained in the discovery file. If it is not, the criminal defense investigator should recommend the information be requested through discovery in a written memorandum to the criminal defense attorney.

Defining Issues During an Investigation

The goals of a criminal defense investigation are often abstract? Simply stated, if the goals were clear, there would be no need for a complete investigation and the endeavor would be reduced to a collection operation only. For example, a goal of an investigation could be to identify the murderer who killed Jane Doe. However, this is not really a goal but rather an agenda encompassing an array of investigative issues that have no real foreseeable end or solution. Issue definition is an abstract endeavor at the micro level of any investigation. Once the investigation is underway, at times, defining an issue can seem difficult at first glance. However, defining each issue faced during an investigation is critical for that investigation to be successful.

If each issue is not defined, a haphazard approach results. In general, any criminal defense investigation is not comprised of just one issue but an array of issues. For example, a witness provides testimony based upon their personal observations of an alleged assault. What issues could exist with this testimony? For example, is the witness credible? Several possible issues could be defined in relation to this witness testimony or any other witness testimony. The goal is a break down the issue into subparts that can be explored through a collection operation and then assessed through analysis.

Where does an "issue" arrive from during a criminal defense investigation? An "issue" is an investigative question that emerges when an information gap is identified. For example, how did the alleged victim arrive at the alleged crime scene? This is an investigative question that requires a specific set of issues to be defined in direct relation to the question. Over the lifespan of a criminal defense investigation, a diverse array of investigative questions will be posed and answered. Initially, these investigative questions will emerge while building a model of the alleged crime. Then, more investigative questions will emerge during the assessment of the hypotheses.[22] The model and hypotheses require information so that they can be assessed.

The following nine-step process should be utilized when attempting to answer an investigative question:

1. What is the defense's question that needs to be answered?

2. Has the defense's question (or similar questions) already been answered by the criminal defense investigator or law enforcement?

3. What are the possible answers to the defense's questions? What alternative explanations should be considered before making a determination?

4. Would the defense's question benefit from structured analysis techniques?

---

[22] See chapters on Hypothesis Generation and Diagnostic Analysis

5. What potential sources of information would be beneficial in answering the defense's questions? Are the sources available?

6. Should the criminal defense investigator seek assistance, information, or expertise while answering the defense's question?

7. Should a brainstorming session be utilized to identify key assumptions?23

---

[23]Adapted from: Richards, H J, and R H Pherson. Structured Analytic Techniques for Intelligence Analysis. 2nd ed. Thousand Oaks: CQ Press, 2015., p 48

Chapter 9

Model Construction

A map is needed to navigate an effective criminal defense investigation; this is referred to as a "model." A criminal defense investigator is faced with an overwhelming amount of information during complex investigations. In many cases, handling these types of investigations is similar to wandering in the fog. You do not find anything unless you trip over it. Unfortunately, this is the approach of many investigators. Their idea of an investigation is to start turning over every rock until they find something of interest, which the investigation then focuses on. This approach is based on tradition and not logical reasoning. In many cases, the traditional approach is highly effective in promoting a single hypotheses. In most cases, this is how the defendant ends up paraded in front of the gallows. The criminal defense investigator must surpass the traditional approach to adequately support the responsible criminal defense attorney.

The information encountered during a criminal defense investigation is similar to a box full of papers with no logical arrangement to ease the discover of the information needed. Often, this is literally the case during a criminal defense investigation. The criminal defense investigator is provided a box full of papers, known as the discovery file. Approaching this file can be akin to utilizing a dictionary out of alphabetical order and being unaware of the meaning of any word in the English language. Many questions immediately arise when considering this box of papers. What is important? How is each document connected? What does each document represent regarding the alleged crime? Typically, sorting and interpreting information contained in the box is based on the experience and intuition of the investigator. Simply stated, this leaves a considerable amount of possibilities to chance.

This book proposes an alternative to the traditional approach of processing information by investigators: the use of a "model" for processing information and knowledge creation or extraction. A model is a representation of an idea, real world conditions, or a system in the world. In many cases, a model describes how a system in the real world will behave. In general, models are used by investigators to interact with, instead of addressing the real system or real world conditions.[24] A model is of special importance to the criminal defense investigator from the standpoint of collections and analysis. A model can be generated in a wide array formats. A model can be generated as a physical model, a tangible representation, a conceptual model, or a mental theoretical concept.[25] A criminal defense investigator will find utility in all types of models depending on the issues faced in each respective case. The subtype of these models can vary widely and are beyond the scope of this book. Generally, considering collection and analysis issues, a conceptual model that is descriptive with components having deterministic, stochastic, and dynamic qualities is extremely beneficial to the criminal defense investigator.

A descriptive model simply describes an idea or concept. For a criminal defense investigator, a descriptive model would describe an alleged crime, a peer-to-peer network, or an investigative methodology. The model can have deterministic or stochastic properties. In some cases, the model may exhibit both properties. Deterministic properties are known relationships within the model. Stochastic properties are attributes of uncertainty.[26] These two types of properties are common in any model utilized by a criminal defense investigator.

---

[24] Clark, Robert M. Intelligence Analysis: a Target-Centric Approach. 3rd ed. Washington: CQ Press, 2010., p. 37

[25] Ibid., p. 38

[26] Ibid.

For example, an alleged crime will always entail an initial known relationship established by the State. The alleged crime will also include relationships or variables that are unknown or denied by the State. On the other hand, all criminal defense investigations are dynamic in nature. Information always undergoes change over the lifetime of the investigation. This is due to the dynamics at play during an investigation, which vary widely from denial and deception to changes in investigative tasks. As a result, any model utilized by a criminal defense investigator will be dynamic in nature. The investigator will add and subtract information from the model over the lifespan of the investigation. A single change in the model will effect the whole model.

The criminal defense investigator utilizes a model in two different respects. First, a model is used to guide the investigator through information collection. In any investigation, the challenge is always determining what information is important enough to allocate investigative resources too. A model can be utilized as an explicate guide in initial collection operations. Second, after the criminal defense investigator has built the model, knowledge extraction can occur. For example, a peer-to-peer network model can be utilized to identify supporting and possible hostile relationships. Without the model, this knowledge would be elusive, but with the model this knowledge can be extracted. Thus, a model assists an investigator during collection operations and during knowledge extraction.

A Model for Criminal Defense

The General Criminal Defense Investigative Model (GCDIM) is applicable to all forms of alleged criminal activity. This model assists the criminal defense investigator to search for and assess information. In general, this model initially acts as a blank template at the onset of a defense investigation. As the defense investigation progress, an actionable model is developed and utilized to extract knowledge.

At the foundation of GCDIM is the Criminal Activity Equation, which is as follows:

$$\textit{Criminal Activity = Intent + Opportunity + Ability}$$

This Criminal Activity Equation demonstrates specifically what variables must exist for an individual to commit a crime. However, the equation does not prove an individual is guilty because they possessed the intent, opportunity, and ability to commit the crime. However, all these variables must be in place for an individual to have committed an alleged crime. In simple terms, if these variables are not in place than the individual is innocent. On the other hand, if these variables are in place, the individual may be guilty. Generally, the alleged presence of these variables is the arena where criminal defense investigations take place.

Intent is a core element of most criminal statutes. This variable is by far the most difficult one to document and measure with a high degree of certainty. In many cases, an individual's intent is measured through physical actions. For example, premeditated murder in most jurisdictions is evident by the accused bring or retrieving the murder weapon throughout the alleged crime. On the other hand, the accused's internal thoughts are measured through statements made to witnesses, in personal writings, and in public outbursts. Thus, intent is a variable that simply refers to what the person intended to accomplish.

One of the most common robust defenses counters is the alibi. This eliminates the opportunity variable. If the accused individual was not in the location of the crime, how did they commit the crime? Simply put, they could not have. However, most criminal defense investigation are by no means this simple. The matter of opportunity can reach levels of complexity far exceeding any Hollywood script. Determining opportunity is a complex process of assessing temporal and geospatial information. Nevertheless, opportunity is simply whether the individual was at the alleged crime scene at the specific time that the crime was committed.

The ability variable is complex and often overlooked during complex criminal cases. The accused's physical ability is directly measured through this variable. For example, could the accused have hid the three-hundred-pound victim's body in an attic? This is a simple scenario but illustrates how this variable directly impacts findings of innocence or guilt.

However, "ability" is not limited to the accused's physical ability, it also takes into account access to physical items, geospatial limitations, and specialized knowledge. Thus, the variable of ability simply refers to whether the accused had the means to commit the alleged crime.

The Criminal Activity Equation is useful as a high-level theoretical lens for assessing criminal activity. However, in practice, it holds limited utility in the area of structured analysis. In general, the primary drawback to the equation is its overly simplistic nature. For example, when considering the Criminal Activity Equation, what specifically should the criminal defense investigator focus on during an investigation? Moreover, what are the primary collection needs for use in analysis? After assessing these questions, the equation's clear lack of utility emerges. Thus, a detailed model is need to provide actionable utility to the Criminal Activity Equation.

The author developed GCDIM to add actionable utility to the Criminal Activity Equation. Actionable Utility is not easily achieved. No "off-the-shelf" models exist and any models purporting simplistic solutions would fail. In general, one persistent issue arises with criminal acts. Every criminal act, and every human act in general, is a completely unique event in time. In theory, a specific criminal act will only occur once in human history. This is why attempts to utilize statistical studies of criminal acts have failed to provide any real actionable utility. In criminal investigations, the generalization of criminal behavior has no real actionable use to criminal investigators or criminal defense investigators.

The lack of an effective "off-the-shelf" model does not preclude the utility of more complex, adaptable models. Because every criminal act is a completely unique event in time, a model needs to be rebuilt and rebuilt with each alleged criminal act. This need to "rebuild" the model on the fly is critical and is fulfilled by using a multipurpose model that is presented as a template, i.e., the model has no data. This form of model presents two advantages. First, the model's empty data structure allows the criminal defense investigator to collect the necessary information to meet the model's data needs. Second, when the criminal defense investigator utilizes the model, the resulting data extraction is based upon information specific to the alleged crime rather than a simplistic generalization. Thus, the model has actionable utility.

GCDIM is based on the Criminal Activity Equation and further expanded with temporal, geospatial, topical, and network data. For clarity, a tree structure is utilized to illustrate GCDIM.

The simplest of forms can be illustrated as follows:

Criminal Act

   Intent or Opportunity or Ability

      Temporal

      Geospatial

      Topical

      Network

This simple model illustrates how information is utilized across the model. With each indentation, a subcategory of the tree is established, which equals a more granular level of detail. However, this simple mode is not very useful as a template. What is needs is a model of explicit information demands. For example, the following underdeveloped model illustrates this approach of explicit information demands:

Alleged Criminal Act

   Opportunity

      Temporal

         What date and time did the criminal act start?

         What date and time did the criminal act end?

      Geospatial

         Where did the criminal act originate?

         Is the criminal act limited to one location?

Where did the criminal act terminate?

Topical

What was the social setting of the criminal act?

Based upon the above example, a model can demand information, which the criminal defense investigator responds to by systematically collecting information to answer each listed question. This example illustrates how actionable utility is generated using a model.

General Criminal Defense Investigative Model

GCDIM is used through the same methodology of responding to a model's information demands. But, how is this model used to exploit information? In general, once the model has been populated to the degree of reflecting real world conditions, which at times will be limited, the information contained in the model is processed through structured analysis. Information exploitation, previously termed "knowledge extraction," is discussed in depth in later chapters.

The model is not intended to be all-encompassing but rather as a template for real world use by a criminal defense investigator. This model is meant to be used from the onset of an investigation until its completion. In many cases, the model will be expanded throughout the investigation's lifecycle. This process of expanding the model is discussed in detail within the discussion on diagnostic analysis presented in later chapters.

The abstract context of a criminal defense investigation requires a model that is scalable based upon the needs of the investigation. The need for scalability is directly tied to the unforeseeable number of witnesses, physical evidence, and many other forms of information that vary from case to case. This scalability is resolved by utilizing a model comprised of components that can be duplicated on an endless scale. Moreover, the components can be organized to represent the underlining network between real-life individuals, locations, and physical evidence. Using these components, a scalable and networked model is possible. The

GCDIM is made up of seven distinct yet interdependent components. These components are depicted in Figure 10.1.

The date/time component (DTC) represents all dates and times documented within the GCDIM and includes temporal data. Moving to the bottom of the model's visual representation, the location component (LC) holds geospatial data. Climbing further up the model, the physical evidence component (PEC), witness component (WC), natural event component (NEC), record component (RC), and analysis component (AC) represent topical data. All of these components combined represent network data. The visual representation is organized to show the interdependency between the components. Essentially, it depicts the components as stacked blocks with the exception of the DTC, which is set vertically, representing the strong date/time aspect that relates to all components. All other components are stacked based upon their theoretical network relationship.

Figure 10.1 - GCDIM

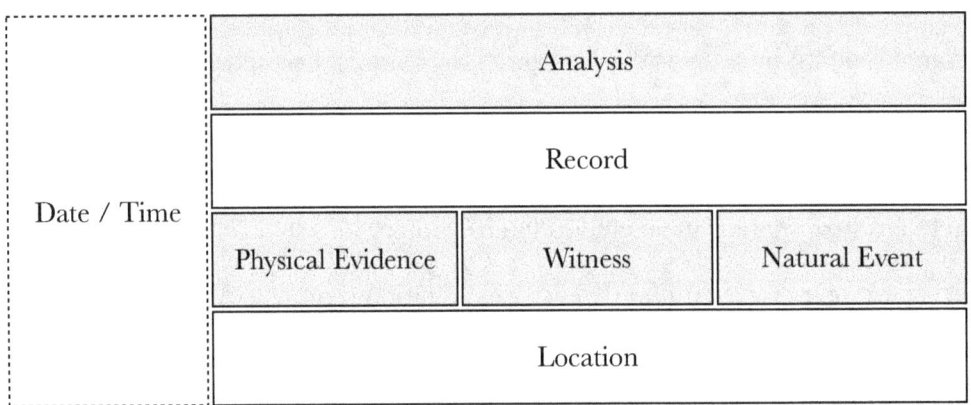

The GCDIM could be made more complex by including an abundance of further components. For clarity and scalability, it has been reduced to its core components. For example, a component representing individual physical actions could be used; however, this has been incorporated in the WC component. Why? Because physical actions can only be made by an individual. Having a separate component would only add unwanted complexity to the model.

For clarity, the GCDIM components are explained in the following descriptions:

Date / Time Component (DTC)

The DTC is an extremely important component. The cause and effect of time on any alleged crime are always intensely examined. The DTC is meant to document all known temporal data. The temporal data will be derived from all forms of information, from witness interviews to telephone records. The key is that the temporal data must have a degree of certainty. If an accurate time is not available, generalized times should be utilized. Typically, one- or two-hour blocks of time should be used. However, all reasonable efforts should be made to reduce these timeframes to a level that has actionable utility. In some cases, however, this may not be possible.

Location Component (LC)

The LC is probably the second most important component of the GCDIM. Generally, geospatial data is viewed in a general sense, for example, the address of a residence. To a limited degree, this is completely adequate. However, when geospatial data is involved, the level of accuracy should be carefully considered and at the forefront of the criminal defense investigator's mind. The difference between where an alleged crime occurred and the location of physical evidence in the alleged crime scene illustrates this need. In some cases, a mere six inches can spell the difference between the evidence proving guilt or innocence. As a general rule, a criminal defense investigator should ensure the highest level of accuracy in geospatial data, when possible. The key is not necessarily where a location is represented by geospatial data but the location in relation to another location point. Thus, the LC is not a physical place but a construct used to determine where a location is in relation to its surrounding environment.

Physical Evidence Component (PEC)

The PEC represents a wide array of information, from trace evidence to large physical items. Essentially, if something exists in the physical world, it is documented through the PEC. For the novice investigator, this is concept can seem abstract. For example, is a dent in a car door physical evidence? Which is the evidence: the car door or the dent? The car door itself is the physical evidence, which by description has a dent. This is an important distinction. Physical evidence is descriptive in nature. In simple terms, the physical item is not important, but its physical condition is important and can only be communicated through a clear description. This is why photographs are so powerful in communicating physical evidence. Thus, the PEC is meant to describe the physical world.

Witness Component (WC)

The WC represents all witnesses involved in the alleged crime. Witnesses include all defendants, alleged victims, law enforcement officers, other first responders, and any other individuals who can provide some level of testimony regarding the alleged crime. The possibilities can vary from eyewitnesses to the medical examiner.

Natural Event Component (NEC)

The NEC is a component that is overlooked during many criminal defense investigations. It will typically not have an impact on an alleged event, but when it does come into play, considerable actionable utility can be gained. The NEC includes any form of weather conditions, the level of light, natural events causing a social impact, space weather or other forms of natural events. Natural events causing a social impact refers to floods, earthquakes, tornados, and hurricanes. Space weather is an under-considered variable, but it does cause an impact on the Earth's surface, specifically, radio communication and other electrical disturbances.

Record Component (RC)

The RC covers a vast amount of possible information. Typically in the area of criminal defense investigation, records are collected from automated systems such as security cameras and telephone records. With limited verification, automated records hold a considerable amount of credibility. On the other hand, the RC also includes records generated by law enforcement personnel, government employees, private companies, and private individuals. These records require robust verification and may be deemed to hold no credibility at times.

Analysis Component (AC)

The AC component may not be present in all criminal defense investigations. The AC deals directly with evidence interpretation by the criminal defense investigator, private entities, and governmental organizations. This includes a wide array of information, from lab reporting to formal analytical products produced by a criminal intelligence analyst or a criminal defense investigator.

The GCDIM Information Network

GCDIM is a networked model. Each component is connected to other components dependent on the interdependency (network) of the information that defines an alleged crime. This networked aspect of GCDIM is another layer of information from which knowledge can be extracted. The components of the GCDIM are enumerated below. Each facet of information that could represent a connection to another component is represented by the symbol "—>" pointing to the specific component.

GCDIM

Date and Time Component (DTC)

1. Start date and time?
2. End date and time?

Location Component (LC)

1. What type of location?

2. What is the specific location?

3. What type of travel is possible at the location?

4. What type of travel is possible in the immediate area?

5. Are roadways or walkways available in the immediate area?

6. What resources are available at the location?

7. Is security (security guards or police force) present at the location?

8. Is physical security (gates, fences, limited access through locked doors) present at the location?

9. What is in the immediate location?

10. Are automated recording devices present? —> RC

11. What is adjacent to the area for immediate access?

12. Are automated recording devices present? —> RC

13. What is adjacent to the area from a medium distance?

14. Are automated recording devices present? —> RC

Witness Component (WC)

1. Who is the witness?

2. What type of witness? (defendant, codefendant, victim, law enforcement, first responder, bystander)

3. Is the witness connected to the alleged crime through physical action?

4. Is the witness connected to physical evidence? —> PEC

5. Is the witness connected to the alleged crime scene? —> LC

6. Is the witness socially connected to other witnesses, co-defendants, or the defendant? —> WC

7. Friends, family, coworker, employee, shared interest, shared belief?

8. Were the witness's actions documented through an automated recording device? —> RC

9. Where was the witness's location in relation to the alleged crime scene? —> LC

10. When did the witness arrive at the alleged crime scene? —> DTC

11. What was the method of travel used to arrive at the alleged crime scene?

12. Is the witness's travel connected with another witness's travel or actions? —> WC

13. Where did the witness travel from before arriving at the alleged crime scene? —> LC

14. Can the witness provide testimony on events that occurred before the alleged crime? —> DTC

    14.1. Is there competing or confirming witness testimony? —> WC

15. What is the witness's testimony specific to the alleged crime?

    15.1. Is there a competing or confirming witness testimony to the above testimony? —> WC

16. When did the witness leave the crime scene? —> DTC

17. What was the method of travel used to leave the alleged crime scene?

18. Is the witness's travel connected with another witness's travel or actions? —> WC

19. Where did the witness travel to from the alleged crime scene? —> LC

20. Can the witness provide testimony on events that followed the alleged crime? —> DTC

    20.1. Is there competing or confirming witness testimony to the above testimony? —> WC

Physical Evidence Component (PEC)

1. What is the physical evidence?

2. Where was the physical evidence located? —> LC

3. At what date and time was the physical evidence found and recovered? —> DTC

4. Who recovered the evidence? —> WC

5. Who is the evidence connected to? —> WC

6. What is the description of the physical evidence?

7.   What does the physical evidence represent in the context of the alleged crime?

8.   Has the evidence been subjected to some form of analysis? —> AC

Record Component (RC)

1.   What type of record is it?

2.   What is the location of the record? —> LC

3.   At what date and time was the record found and recovered? —> DTC

4.   Who found and recovered the record? —> WC

5.   Who held custody of the record before recovery? —> WC

6.   Who is the record connected to? —> WC

7.   What is the content of the record?

8.   What does the record represent regarding the context of the alleged crime?

9.   Has the record been subjected to some form of analysis? —> AC

Natural Event Component (NEC)

1.   Did any natural events occur? —> LC

2.   What date and time did they occur? —> DTC

3.   What was the location of the natural event? —> LC

4.   Do any images of the event exist? —> RC

5.   Has an analysis of natural event been completed? —> AC

6.   Is there a witness to the natural event? —> WC

Analysis Component (AC)

1.   What type of analysis has been conducted?

2.   What is the content of the analysis? —> DTC | PEC | WC | NEC | RC

3.   At what date and time was the analysis completed? —> DTC

4.   Who completed the analysis? —> WC

5.   What does the analysis represent in the context of the alleged crime?

Utilizing the GCDIM

At first glance, utilizing the GCDIM can seem overwhelming. However, the model is not meant to be utilized in the form presented above. The application of GCDIM will vary from one criminal defense investigator to the next. The model can be built into a paperwork system or a database. Ideally, the model should be represented in two forms. First, it should be represented in the narrative reporting generated by the criminal defense investigator, which is used by the criminal defense investigator and the criminal defense attorney. Second, the model should be represented in a network chart. Although, all facets of information cannot be illustrated in this chart, the network itself should be represented in a simple visual depiction. No matter the how GCDIM is applied, the documentation generated through the use of GCDIM should be usable and complete in a manner that meets the criminal defense investigator's personal work preferences. The information contained within GCDIM is meant to be utilized in structured analytical techniques. Thus, the ability to retrieve information from GCDIM is critical.

Chapter 10

Key Assumption Check

During any investigation or general analysis, we subconsciously or intentionally make what are referred to as key assumptions. Recognizing that we make assumptions is a critical factor during any investigation. If we do not recognize that assumptions are being made, we stand a chance of having a critical failure of the overall investigation. A key assumption check should be completed at the onset of any criminal defense investigation and on a recurring basis throughout the investigation. Moreover, the criminal defense investigator should determine any assumptions made by the State during the initial stages of an investigation.

Defining a Key Assumption

A key assumption is an assumption that has a critical impact on the investigation. If a key assumption is incorrect, the whole investigation will collapse. For example, a common key assumption made by investigators is the credibility of a witness. We assume the witness has good eyesight, hearing, and the ability to detect odors. If this key assumption is incorrect, the witness's testimony should be discarded. If we hold to the key assumption the witness is able to make an observation and provide credible testimony and this key assumption is incorrect, the resulting investigative conclusion will be erroneous.

A key assumption can be made in many forms, from taking a witness's testimony at face value to assumptions that a human being is able to perform a specific physical action. In simple terms, key assumptions made during an investigation can create a critical investigative failure. All key assumptions made during an investigation must be articulated in a formal, structured process. This process is referred to as a key assumption check.

The first and critical step of completing a key assumption check is admitting that an assumption is being made. In practice, this requires a criminal defense investigator to exercise a high degree of self-discipline. All aspects of the investigation must be objectively reviewed and assessed for assumptions.

In addition to key assumption, key unknowns exist within a case. In simple terms, a key unknown refers to information that is unknown or denied. In theory, a key unknown is the opposing theoretical view of a key assumption. A key unknown is comprised of information that is truly unknown for any number of reasons. This information may be at the time denied by the State or unattainable by the criminal defense investigator. In either case, the information is simply unknown. A key unknown is not silent evidence; it is information known to exist that is unattainable. The criminal defense investigator must account for this unknown information recognizing the key unknown's potential to force a change in the investigation at a later junction or cause a critical failure.

Like a key assumption, the existence of a key unknown is detrimental to the overall analysis work conducted by a criminal defense investigator. If a key unknown is ignored during the investigation, the whole investigation is subject to the risk of collapse. Discerning the difference between a key assumption and key unknown can be confusing. Fully understanding the difference is critical during the application of a key assumption check. A key assumption is a true assumption made by the criminal defense investigator that is logically sound. On the other hand, a key unknown is specific information that is completely unknown to the criminal defense investigator and no reasonable assumption can be made to fill the information gap. Thus, the key unknown has a higher probability of causing an investigative failure. Ideally, a key unknown should be eliminated through further investigation, but this may not always be possible.

The Key Assumption Check Method

A key assumption check is completed through the following steps:

1. Determine all current assumptions being made during the investigation by challenging all investigative interpretations of alleged events.

2. Is there evidence to support each interpretation?

3. Has each interpretation been challenged through field investigation?

4. Is there an opposing interpretation by another investigator or interested party?

5. Is it possible to hold an opposing interpretation?

6. Does corroborating evidence exists to support the interpretation?

7. After identifying all assumptions, assess each assumption through the following questions:

8. Why is the assumption being made?

9. In what circumstances could the assumption be wrong?

10. What is the confidence level of the assumption?

11. Could any emerging evidence impact the assumption and make the assumption invalid?

12. If the assumption turns out to be invalid, what impact will this have on investigative conclusions?

13. Organize the assumptions into the following three categories:

14. Reasonably solid

15. Correct with some caveats

16. Unsupported—the "key unknowns"

17. Convert any key unknowns into investigative priorities.27

---

27 Adapted from: Richards, H J, and R H Pherson. Structured Analytic Techniques for Intelligence Analysis. 2nd ed. Thousand Oaks: CQ Press, 2015., p. 211-212

Key Assumption Check in Practice

The key assumption check brings an important question to the table, relevant to both for-profit or public investigations: Why would an investigator make assumptions? Theoretically, an investigator should never make an assumption. Many professional and public investigators will argue their work product does not contain any assumptions; however, upon close examination, this is simply not true. Reflecting on the previous example, how many investigators confirm an eyewitness is capable of making the alleged observation? This form of confirmation is rare in professional and public investigations. Why would an assumption be made about an eyewitness's ability to observe an incident? In most circumstances, this form of assumption is based upon solid logical reasoning. An eyewitness whose observations are made during daylight and in close proximity is an example of a logical, sound assumption of the witness's ability to make those observations. On the other hand, if the witness had made the same observations during low-light conditions from a greater distance than the same assumption would be considerably less sound. The first scenario presents an assumption categorized as "correct with some caveats." The caveat is the possibility that the witness is dependent on eyeglasses, which may have or may not have been worn during the observations. The second scenario differs considerably from the first. In this scenario, the witness is making the same observations during low-light conditions at a greater distance. The assumption in this scenario would be categorized as "unsupported." There are just to many unanswered questions to make a logically sound assumption regarding the witnesses capability of making those observations. The key question in both scenarios is whether the witness"s observations are detrimental to the investigation.

Analysis in a criminal defense investigation requires a micro-level approach to information. This micro approach is a critical aspect in applying a key assumption check. Overly broad assumptions are highly problematic and carry an extreme liability of failure. Continuing the witness example above, are the witness's observations detrimental to the investigation? This is an important question, and the answer can be used to differentiate between an assumption and a key assumption. However, a simplistic example will not demonstrate how to make this judgement. The assumption has to be weighed against the entire alleged incident. What do the witness's observations prove? What impact does this proof have on the overall alleged criminal act? The impact of any evidence and its underlining assumptions has to be taken into account using a holistic approach.

Every criminal defense investigation will be comprised of at least some key assumptions. The goal is to determine which assumptions are key in the investigation and to assess the underlining evidence supporting those assumptions. The identification and evaluation of key assumptions is critical to prevent possible failure. Moreover, the identification of key unknowns through a key assumption check allows the investigator to close investigative gaps that are detrimental to the overall investigation.

Chapter 11

Information Quality Check

When new information is received during an investigation, an information quality check should be completed. The instinctive practice of the criminal defense investigator should ensure that this structured analysis technique is applied to all information. This method should be built into the criminal defense investigator's entire collection and analysis process. In general, an information quality check ensures a degree of certainty in regard to the quality and credibility of information. This method is not complex, but it is meant to be used as a reoccurring theme during an investigation. A criminal defense investigator will spend a large portion of their investigative career completing information quality checks.

The Concept of an Information Quality Check

An information quality check is applied by testing the credibility of information. This process, in simple terms, is a matter of fact checking. At times, this fact check requires specialized knowledge and training. The information tested can range from complex scientific information to a simple address. This process's main focuses is on credibility, but it will also lead to the identification of new collection needs that may produce additional information.

In the range of information commonly confronted by a criminal defense investigator, this method is not normally overly complex. During a typical analysis project, the criminal defense investigator will be confronted by witness testimony, law-enforcement reporting, and investigative methodologies employed by law enforcement. This information must be rigorously tested for credibility as a matter of practice. For example, all witness statements should be tested for credibility in terms of the testimony content. This can range from environmental conditions to the witness's physical capabilities. The key factor of an information quality check is the method employed. In simple terms, when the criminal defense investigator is confronted with new information, the method is utilized. When old information is challenged, the method is utilized once again in light of the investigator's maturing understanding of the information, based on the new information. Thus, an information quality check is repeatedly employed.

The typical information encountered by a criminal defense investigator that requires an information quality check includes the following:

1. Law enforcement reporting

2. Law enforcement procedures and policies

3. Search warrants

4. Forensic testing

5. Witness testimonies

6. Investigative methodologies

The above list is not exhaustive but rather a general guideline. Basic information, for example, an address, should always be verified for accuracy. The goal is to achieve a high degree of certainty regarding the information utilized during an investigation.

Each of the above forms of information require specialized knowledge. The process of testing search warrant affidavits through an information quality check differs from the process used when assessing law enforcement procedures. There is no standard way of applying an information quality check. The process will vary depending on the information. However, the overall goal is to confirm whether the information is correct and credible.

Law Enforcement Reporting

Considering the environment the criminal defense investigator operates within, law enforcement reporting is of special interest. This specific information should be the first information placed under an information quality check. Law enforcement reporting varies from agency to agency. However, generally, all law enforcement reporting is presented in a narrative format. Otherwise, individual identifying information is typically presented in a form-based report. This report will include specific information, such as the location of the alleged crime and other data that is used by the law enforcement agency for management purposes.

The narrative of law enforcement reporting is of special consideration for the criminal defense investigator. This narrative will describe the reporting officer's observations and actions. The narrative will include how the reporting officer arrived at the alleged scene, their initial observations, statements made to the reporting officer by witnesses and suspects, the reporting officer's investigative actions, and the final result of the reporting officer's actions. In most cases, this narrative represents a wealth of information for the criminal defense investigator.

Placing law enforcement reporting under an information quality check will vary depending on the alleged crime. However, the main focus should be on descriptions of locations, physical items, and individual testimony included in the reporting. Law enforcement officers are trained to provide detailed descriptive narratives of their observations and investigative efforts. These descriptive narratives include times, dates, and descriptions in regard to the size, location, and appearance of physical objects and individuals. In many cases, the reporting law enforcement officer will fail to provide an accurate description, or their own bias will be apparent in their reporting.

All dates, times, measurements, and physical descriptions should be compared to other available sources. These sources include reporting from non-law enforcement agencies, law enforcement administrative documentation (dispatch logs, time cards, and other forms of administrative documentation not maintained in the case file), photographs, video footage, and information collected by the criminal defense investigator. The goal is to confirm the information presented in law enforcement reporting through an independent source. Ideally, several independent sources should be examined to the extent of available sources.

Checking the quality of law enforcement reporting provides two results. First, the criminal defense investigator is able to confirm the accuracy of the information. Second, the falsehoods and inaccurate information uncovered through the information quality check can be used by the defense attorney to impeach the reporting law enforcement officer during trial. All falsehoods and inaccurate information should be clearly communicated to the responsible attorney in a written report. Generally, the best practice is to write a report on each specific issue by clearly stating the falsehoods or inaccurate information presented in the law enforcement reporting and then clearly stating the correct information, as well as how the correct information was uncovered and its source.

Law Enforcement Procedures and Policies

All policies and procedures used by the investigating law enforcement agency should be examined in detail. This is approached much like law enforcement reporting. Law enforcement agencies can to a large degree develop their own policies and procedures as they see fit. However, their policies and procedures must be based upon acceptable practices. There are known and accepted ways of performing an investigation, and then there are unacceptable ways.

Typically, contemporary law enforcement policies and procedures are based upon a template provided by a recognized authority. Sometimes this recognized authority is the State's top-tier law enforcement agency, for example, a state police agency. On the other hand, the template may have been provided by an independent agency involved in policy development, for example, the International Association of Chiefs of Police (IACP). In the worst case scenario, the law enforcement agency develops its own policies and procedures.

However, this is less common in contemporary society, considering the overwhelming number of resources available from independent, supporting agencies.

Reviews of most policies and procedures used by law enforcement agencies include minimal detail, unless the policy and procedure deals with a critical issue such as the use of force. Policies and procedures can be placed in one of two categories: first, those dealing with administrative issues such as officer appearance and conduct and, second, those dealing with operational issues such the processing of crime scenes. Operational policies tend to be shorter in detail compared to administrative policies and procedures. This is especially true on the issue of how a criminal investigation is conducted.

All policies and procedures applicable to the alleged crime should be examined and compared to the investigating officer's conduct. Did the investigating officer adhere the agency's policies and procedures? In the author's experience, making these comparisons is typically frustrating due the lack of detail in agencies' policies and procedures. On the other hand, when strict procedures govern the actions of the investigating officer, errors on the part of that officer can be fruitful for the defense. For example, an agency's chain of custody policy is an area where errors can sometimes be found; these are directly tied to the assessment of the evidence's credibility. Typically, law enforcement agencies circumvent officer errors by utilizing simple policies and procedures in their criminal investigations. However, strict adherence to the overly simple policies and procedures does not validate an officer's investigative conduct. The officer's actions still must be acceptable in comparison to known and recognized standards.

Fortunately, law enforcement agencies have recognized standards developed by the highest authority on the subject of law enforcement, the U.S. Government. Typically, these are the most detailed standards in the areas of evidence handling, forensic practices, and crime scene processing. To adequately assess the quality of an investigative officers actions, the criminal defense investigator should be adequately familiar with these standards. For example, the publication titled *Crimes Scene Investigation: A Guide for Law Enforcement*[28] is an excellent source to gauge the results of a crime scene investigation completed by law enforcement. The publication is in its third edition as of the writing of this book. In the first edition, an interesting perspective on the publication's background is presented.

NIJ was asked by Attorney General Janet Reno in 1995 to study cases in which convicted sex offenders were later exonerated by DNA testing. This study resulted in the 1996 publication, Convicted by Juries, Exonerated by Science: Case Studies in the Use of DNA Evidence to Establish Innocence After Trial. After being briefed on this publication, Attorney General Reno asked NIJ to develop a consistent approach to the processing of crime scenes. As a result, NIJ initiated the Technical Working Group on Crime Scene Investigation to develop recommended practices for crime scene management.[29]

The above quote alone should cause the criminal defense investigator to closely examine the policies and procedures utilized by law enforcement agencies. Many U.S. Government documents exist that can be used to fully assess the procedures and methods utilized by an investigating officer. However, the criminal defense investigator should not limit their examination to publications by the U.S. Government. There are many active researchers in the area of criminal investigative practices from an array of disciplines. Criminal defense investigators should stay abreast of emerging research that has undergone peer review. In many cases, this research can be beneficial and at times, it can become more valuable than any governmental publication.

Checking the quality of the policies and procedures utilized by an investigating officer allows the criminal defense investigator to determine if the investigative methods used were acceptable. Any conflict should be clearly reported in writing to the defense attorney. This report should include a description of the conflict based upon the specific action, a clear source for the evidence of this action, and supporting documentation of the conflict; this information should be made available to the attorney in a digestible form.

---

[28] National Institute of Justice (U.S.). Technical Working Group on Crime Scene Investigation. Crime Scene Investigation, 2013.

[29] Ibid., p. 3

Search Warrants

Search warrants are a common instrument utilized by law enforcement to uncover evidence. The process of obtaining a search warrant is based upon submitting a written application to a judicial official. This application or affidavit is a potential weak point in the process and should be carefully reviewed by the criminal defense investigator.

There is no standard way of preparing a written application for a search warrant. The style of the document will vary from investigator to investigator. The key element of this document is the content communicated to the judicial official and the requested limits of the search. For one, the document should adequately describe the location to be searched. At times, errors are made in this description. Second, the application should describe the limits of the search warrant, which refer to how the search will take place and what evidence will be searched for and seized. Once a search warrant application is approved, the investigating officer is limited to the scope of the original request, unless an additional search warrant is obtained. In some cases, these limits will be violated during the search.

During the criminal defense investigator's review of the search warrant affidavit, careful attention must be given the to the location authorized for the search and the limits of the search and seizure. Any actions that differed from the scope of the search warrant affidavit should be focused upon and clearly reported to the defense attorney in writing. This report should include information from the search warrant affidavit that is in conflict with the actions of the investigating officer, which should be well documented and sourced.

Forensic Testing

Forensic testing is becoming more common in criminal investigations and is a complex topic that is constantly evolving due to widespread academic research interests in this area. Many criminal investigations will not utilize any form of forensic testing. Typically, more common crimes such as burglary, assault, and petty crimes will not be investigated through forensic testing. On the other hand, major crimes such as murder and rape will more commonly include some form of forensic testing. The criminal defense investigator needs to have a working knowledge of forensic testing that of a normal criminal investigator.

From a criminal defense investigator's perspective, forensic testing should be viewed from two different perspectives:the process utilized to collect and preserve the physical evidence and the process utilized to test or examine the physical evidence. These two perspectives together should form the foundation of the criminal defense investigator's review of any forensic testing.

The collection and preservation should be closely examined. A considerable amount of material is available as the basis for this examination. The first material considered should be any literature available from the lab providing the testing service. Typically, the lab will have some form of literature on the collection and preservation of a specific type of evidence. For example, the FBI laboratory publishes an in-depth publication on the collection, preservation, and submission of evidence, titled *Handbook of Forensic Services*.[30] Second, academic, peer-reviewed articles should be considered, especially in the case of emerging forensic tests.

Apart from collection and preservation, the specific forensic testing technique should be examined. This review can be complex and to a large degree requires a specialized education. Ideally, an expert in the specific testing method would be utilized to complete the review, but this type of resource will only be available in limited cases. The criminal defense investigator can make a limited review of the forensic testing. For one, is the lab involved in the testing credible? Many criminal labs have been found to be less than credible in the past, and the specific lab may have a current controversy that challenges the lab's credibility. Does the forensic scientist have the necessary credentials to complete the testing? All credentials should be verified to the fullest existent possible. Are the testing results accurately applied in the context of the investigation? In simple terms, is the forensic testing being misrepresented in regard to application and interpretation? Some forensic testing proves a fact but has no

---

[30] Laboratory, FBI. Handbook of Forensic Services. Justice Department, 2004.

real utility, for example, biological testing to determine the presence of blood on a murder victim. Does this form of testing really have any utility in proving guilt or innocence? Many times, forensic testing does nothing but muddy the water due to an overzealous investigating officer who fails to understand the application and interpretation of the specific test. Reviewing forensic testing can be a complex endeavor. Fortunately, a criminal defense investigator will observe a group of recurring forensic tests during their career. Acceptable practices, the application and interpretation, and available peer review academic articles regarding this core group of forensic testing should be highly familiar to the criminal defense investigator.

Forensic testing encompasses an array of scientific and technical disciplines. Today, forensic testing includes various areas, from hard science applications to the examination of digital electronic applications and related networks. New testing techniques are always emerging and appearing in criminal investigations. The criminal defense investigator should always be aware of these emerging applications in forensic testing. Unfortunately, some so-called forensic techniques are nothing more than junk science. This is a critical subject and one that can have destructive results on the foundations of criminal justice. Over time, these techniques are identified and debunked in court. However, this is only done through the handwork of legal and other professionals. The practicing criminal defense investigator should be well read on emerging techniques and those being challenged in court.

Any identified conflict with the forensic testing should be clearly communicated to the defense attorney in writing. Both a written report and any available supporting source material should be prepared for the defense attorney on each specific issue. Not only does the criminal defense investigator need to understand forensic testing issues, the defense attorney must also understand these issues in detail. The importance of delivering high quality source material on identified issues cannot be overstated.

Witness Testimony

Handling and assessing witness testimony is a key theme during any criminal defense investigation. In some cases, the handling of witnesses is the primary focus of a criminal defense investigator during limited investigations. In large complex investigations, the handling and assessing of witness testimony can consume a considerable amount of time and resources. As a result, the ability of a criminal defense investigator to determine the quality of a specific witness's testimony is a critical skill.

Witnesses emerge in a wide array of forms. Everyone other than the defendant is a possible witness, and for someone to be a witness they must have some form of knowledge specifically related to the alleged crime. Both factors must be in place for someone to be a viable witness. Why is the defendant not viewed as a witness? In simple terms, the court is unable to compel the defendant to provide testimony, but anyone else can be forced to testify.

Witness testimony should be assessed for quality on three fronts: first, the content of the witness's testimony, second, the witness's ability to have acquired adequate knowledge to provide their testimony, which is one of the most commonly overlooked issues, and lastly, the witness's possible bias should be considered. How are they socially connected to other witnesses? These three aspects are used to measure the quality of a specific witness's testimony, which equals their credibility as a witness.

The content of witness's testimony is another critical aspect. In simple terms, this content is what makes them a witness. Unfortunately, in most cases, a group of witnesses will not give consistent testimonies. There is almost always a variation from witness to witness. This should be expected. The key factor to remember is that a witness makes observations independently from their peers. For example, one witness's vision may be obstructed and limited compared to that of another witness. Two witnesses may have viewed the same incident from different timelines. In turn, these witnesses will provide testimony that differs. The key to assessing these two testimonies is based on what they should be able to testify to compared to what they may be interpreting from their observations. This single distinction is why it is paramount to interview all witnesses, even when law enforcement has already documented testimony separating a witness's true observations from their interpretation of events. Moreover, each witness should be assessed regarding how their testimony has changed from when they were first interviewed by law enforcement to the interview completed by the criminal defense investigator. In the end, the investigator should understand the comparisons between specific witness's testimony and that of their peers, as well as the true limitations of that testimony.

Witnesses can provide testimony based upon five senses: ophthalmoception (sight), audioception (hearing), gustaoception (taste), olfacoception (smell), and tactioception (touch). Moreover, a witness is able to perceive their environment through other forms of stimuli such as temperature, kinesthetics, pain, balance, and vibration. Typically, a witness will provide testimony based upon more than one sense. Most commonly, a criminal defense investigator will encounter witnesses whose testimonies are based upon sight and hearing. The most common form of witness testimony is based upon sight, referred to as "eyewitness testimony," with segments of testimony based upon their hearing.

The most common issue confronted by criminal defense investigators in relation to eyewitnesses is the witness's ability to have observed a specific event. This is also the most commonly overlooked issue when examining eyewitness testimony. At first glance, this seems to be an issue that does not require scrutiny. However, in many cases, eyewitness accounts are substandard due to the limited ability of human vision within a specific environment. A classic example is an observation made by a key witness in low-light conditions. Thus, an eyewitness's testimony should be examined in detail in relation to the environment where the observations occurred.

Like that of an eyewitness, all forms of testimony based upon human sensory abilities should be closely examined. For each sense, the witness's ability to have adequately gained the knowledge underpinning their testimony should be questioned. All forms of human sensory ability are unique, requiring specialized knowledge to access them and prove if the witness's testimony is in fact misleading. The criminal defense investigator should be well educated on the most common aspects of human senses and how to generate evidence to prove or disprove a witness's testimony. In general, the proving or disproving of a witness's ability to have observed a specific event is gained through scientific testing. For example, when testing an eyewitness's ability have observed an event in low-light conditions, a vision study is utilized; this is a technique used by forensic photographers. Testing the witness's ability to have observed the event is a matter of witness credibility. Unfortunately, many times this approach is overlooked by criminal defense investigators.

Bias is an all-too-common reality in witness testimony. A criminal defense investigator must be sensitive to the possibility of a witness holding some level of bias. This is especially true in cases of more serious criminal allegations such as murder or crimes of a sexual nature. At times, a witness's biases will be overtly apparent, and the witness may even admit to their bias. How a witness describes people and places is typically a good indicator of possible basis, for example, a witness's description of another race or religion or use of slang terms to describe an area, like "ghetto" or "slum." On the other hand, a witness's biases may not be readily apparent. Social connections between witnesses and the defendant can play a dangerous role in witness testimony. A witness may have intentions or preconceived views based upon these social connections. A witness's family, friends, and professional connections can impact their testimony to the extant of withholding or providing misleading information. This may be rooted in good intentions, malicious intent, or in some form of perceived defense of their self or another party. Moreover, a witness may present an unknown bias in the form of a pre-conceived view of the defendant or based upon a prior negative event with the defendant. A witness may use their testimony as an opportunity for retribution. The criminal defense investigator should always be open to possibility of bias and its impact on witness testimony.

Any factor impacting the quality of a witness's testimony should be clearly reported to the defense attorney in writing. The report should clearly describe the specific issue impacting the witness's testimony and related known supporting evidence. In many cases, a

134

Criminal defense investigator will need to uncover additional evidence to support these claims.

Investigative Methodology

A criminal defense investigator is not just an investigator utilized by an attorney but also an advisor on criminal investigation. This is the core knowledge applied by a criminal defense investigator. After considering all forms of information relayed in writing, media, or verbal communication, the next key area to apply an information quality check is on the criminal investigation completed by law enforcement. In simple terms, the original law enforcement investigation process is considered standalone information to be reviewed and examined by the criminal defense investigator. This form of information quality check can be captured in two questions: What occurred during the law enforcement investigation of the alleged crime? What did not occur during the investigation? By comparing the answers to these two questions using an in-depth knowledge of criminal investigation, a criminal defense investigator is applying an information quality check.

This form of information quality check requires an in-depth understanding of criminal investigation. This cannot be overstated. The criminal defense investigator must not only understand the process of criminal investigation but also have in-depth applied knowledge. Without this, the information quality check will be nothing more than a failed endeavor highlighted by self-assurance born out of ignorance.

The first step in examining a completed criminal investigation is attempting to understand, to the furthest degree possible, why each investigative action was taken or not taken. This allows the criminal defense investigator to understand why certain witnesses were interviewed, certain evidence was collected, and other investigative tasks were conducted. This is not only a matter of applying an information quality check but is also intended to uncover the State's criminal theory. The incompetence or inexperience of law enforcement investigators can limit the effectiveness of this endeavor, making law enforcement investigative efforts appear abstract or illogical. At a minimum, all law enforcement investigative actions should be uncovered and documented.

After understanding, or at least determining the full extent of, law enforcement investigative efforts, the investigation as a whole should be assessed for possible failures and errors. This is a matter of judging the credibility of the law enforcement investigation. The criminal defense investigator must apply learned knowledge of criminal investigation to achieve this goal. Were there witnesses that were not interviewed and should have been? Is documentation missing that should be available for review? Did law enforcement investigators fail to collect physical evidence or even fail to attempt collection? Has appropriate forensic testing not been completed on the physical evidence? Has critical information been ignored? These types of questions will vary depending on the circumstances and type of the alleged crime. Thus, the criminal defense investigator must be knowledgeable about the criminal investigation methods used in the specific alleged crime.

Any failures or errors uncovered in the law enforcement investigation should be clearly reported to the defense attorney in writing. The law enforcement investigator acting in error, or failing to act, must be supported with law enforcement training documentation, authoritative literature, or the qualified expert testimony of the criminal defense investigator.

Chapter 12

Chronology Analysis

Any criminal act can be reduced to a simple chronology. In simple terms, a chronology is a series of events organized by time. In a criminal defense investigation, a chronology has considerable utility. The criminal defense investigator is able to determine when an event occurred in comparison to events that occurred before and after the event, as well as the relation of events to locations, individuals, and the context of events. A chronology of an alleged crime acts as a storyboard from which considerable insight can be gained.

Unfortunately, the work environment of a criminal defense investigator is complex and requires the processing of a considerable of amount of information in a wide array of forms. This information can be composed of witness statements, telephone records, security camera footage, and many other forms of information. All this information has to be composed into a clear image of the incident. A chronology is utilized to construct this image.

Constructing a chronology is a straightforward process. Typically, the information initially received by the criminal defense investigator when accepting the case will be the starting point. During the onset of the investigation, all information is sorted based upon the date and time of occurrence. This information is then placed on a horizontal axis in chronological order, typically starting from left to right with the most recent event at the end of the axis. During this systematic process of placing the information in chronological order, the quality of the information should be considered.

Information used in the chronology will be received in many different forms. It can typically be categorized as high or low quality. In the construction of a chronology, high quality information is information that has been documented in association with a date and time value, for example, security camera footage, telephone records, and digital images. This form of information is easily organized in chronological order with a high degree of confidence after confirming the validity of the timestamp. On the other hand, low quality information presents several problems. Low quality information is information that is not normally documented in association with a date and time value, for example, witness testimony of the times specific events occurred. This is the most common form of low quality information in the construction of a chronology. In short, human beings are not well equipped to recall precise times that specific events occurred. In turn, consideration must be utilized when placing this type of low quality information on the chronology axis. In practice, low quality information should be viewed as approximate rather than precise.

Constructing a Chronology

A considerable amount of information will be assessed by a criminal defense investigator throughout a criminal defense investigation in order to construction a chronology. The following questions should be used systematically in assessing the resulting chronology:

- Is there a significant temporal distance between events? Is there a possibility of a gap in the available information?
- Is there a geographical distance between events? Does the geographical distance align with the available time for travel or other associated actions?
- Is there information that may have had an impact on or could be related to the event that has not been included?
- Is there an alternative explanation for each event in the timeline? Are there events in the timeline that are unrelated to the alleged crime?
- Does the timeline contain all the events that make up the alleged crime?
- What are the information gaps?

- Are there any segments of the timeline where new information can be collected in the present?

- Are there any information gaps that should have been met by the law enforcement investigation? Why? Is it possible law enforcement ignored the information? If the alleged crime occurred, why does this information not exist? Is the absence of information proof of innocence?

- Are there events not included in the timeline that could have influenced the alleged crime?[31]

The above questions should be systematically worked through when constructing a chronology. In practice, the chronology constructed during a criminal defense investigation will be revised each time new information is uncovered. Initially, a considerable amount of information will be used to construct the chronology; this will be derived from the initial discovery materials received from the defense attorney. Then, additional information will be plotted on the chronology as it is uncovered during the criminal defense investigation and updates to the discovery material are received.

Information gaps are expected during an investigation, and all attempts should be made to close these gaps. Significant temporal distances between two adjacent chronological events indicate an information gap. However, it is necessary to ask to what degree a temporal distance is significant. This question is directly tied to the context of the adjacent chronological events. For example, two gunshots are reported five minutes apart at the same location. This is a significant temporal distance, considering the two gunshots could be tied to the same incident or two separate incidents. In order to determine if the gunshots are part of a common incident, further information will be need. Thus, a gap in information exists that requires further collection. On the other hand, if the two gunshots were only seconds apart, the temporal distance would be less significant.

Determining if a specific temporal distance is significant requires focused critical thinking. A criminal defense investigator must weigh all training, education, and experience

---

[31] Adapted from: Richards, H J, and R H Pherson. Structured Analytic Techniques for Intelligence Analysis. 2nd ed. Thousand Oaks: CQ Press, 2015., p. 211-212

on the specific temporal event and how it relates to all adjacent temporal events. In simple terms, the criminal defense investigator must utilize his or her general knowledge and determine specifically how much temporal distance should exist between adjacent temporal events. The distances could be significant if they are too long or too short in duration. The key is analyzing the adjacent temporal events as individual events and then as competing events.

- Is there a geographical distance between events? Does the geographical distance align with the available time for travel or other associated actions?
- Is there information that has not been included that may have had an impact on or could be related to the event?
- Is there an alternative explanation for each event in the timeline? Are there events that belong to an unrelated timeline in respect to the alleged crime?
- Does the timeline have all the events that makeup the alleged crime?
- What are the information gaps?
- Are there any segments of the timeline where new information can be collected in a contemporary setting?
- Are there any information gaps that should have been met by the law enforcement investigation? Why? Is it possible law enforcement ignored the information? If the alleged crime is true, why does this information not exist? Is the absence of information proof of innocents?
- Is there events outside the timeline that could influenced the alleged crime?[32]

Utilizing Investigative Information

Time sensitive information is used during the assembly of a chronology. This information is the foundation of any chronology. Data derived from video footage, photographs, written logs, official reporting, and other forms of documentation holding valid temporal values are useful assembling the chronology. However, a criminal defense investigator should always consider of the credibility of the data. If possible, all temporal

---

[32]Ibid.

data should be verified. For example, the date and timestamp of security camera footage should always be verified by examining a live recording. Typically, a display screen is available where the date and time can be observed and compared to a known, accurate date and time. If any temporal data if found to be inaccurate, it should be documented along with its supporting evidence. In turn, the data should be adjusted before it is included in the chronology. Appropriate annotations should be made on the chronology indicating these adjustments.

The following temporal data sources are common in a chronology:

• Security camera footage

• Law enforcement dispatch logs and reporting

• EMS dispatch logs and reporting

• Telephone records

• Witness testimony containing a temporal component

Additional investigative information can be included in the chronology. Geospatial data should also be included when dealing with more than one location. Travel time between locations can play an important role when considering the defendant's ability to commit a crime. Moreover, topical data can be useful in limited cases. Short descriptions of each event that also reference other investigative data can play an important role in understanding a chronology. Brief descriptions of witness observations springboard the analysis of witness credibility.

Assembling and Reporting the Chronology

Chronologies are a powerful tool in communication. This includes communication between the defense Investigator and the attorney. This also includes the attorney's communication with the court. Generally, a complex chronology is assembled by the criminal defense investigator during the initial stages as information emerges. Then, over time, information is removed from the chronology that is found to have no utility in understanding the event in question. The best practice is to use all available data then remove data as needed.

During the initial stages of assembling a chronology, a single credible point in time should be selected as the initial staring point. From this point, the chronology should be assembled forward in time and back in time. The initial starting point should approximately fall in the middle range of the chronology's span. The initial temporal data generated from law enforcement is generally adequate for this purpose. The documentation generated from a 911 call or law enforcement dispatch logs will contain temporal documentation. The goal is to use an accurate temporal data point that the criminal defense investigator has a high degree of confidence in.

Chronologies can be assembled in any form depending on the issue at hand. A chronology can consist of a simple horizontal line with just a few vertical lines representing independent events. On the other hand, a chronology can grow to be multi-tiered, where multiple chronologies are represented allowing a comparison between parallel chronologies. The final chronology or chronologies should be specifically prepared to meet the demands of the investigation. This can only be judged on a case by case bases. The Criminal Activity Equation should also be utilized when finalizing the chronology or chronologies:

Criminal Activity = Intent + Opportunity + Ability

The final chronology is reported to the attorney. At times, more than one chronology will be needed to show different facets of an event. As a general rule, a chronology should be made as simple as possible without redacting the overall narrative of the subject event.

Sophisticated computer software is available to assist in the assembly of a chronology. However, computer software should be utilized with caution. At best, computer software is only a means to capture temporal data and then display the information. Even though temporal data includes quantitative variables, the underlining cause and effect demonstrated through the chronology is of a qualitative nature. Simply stated, contemporary computer software is currently ill suited to handle this form of analysis. The criminal defense investigator must perform the qualitative analysis through critical thinking, framed by the process described above.

A chronology is a robust instrument in any criminal defense investigation. The aggregation of temporal data from multiple sources allows the criminal defense investigator to complete a comparative study of information representing an event. Through the process of assembling a chronology, relationships between independent events or timelines can be uncovered.

Chapter 13

Network Analysis

Investigative data can be viewed from many varying angles. A beneficial one is how information within an event is connected. How do relationships between witnesses emerge? How are witnesses connected to places and durations of time? A criminal defense investigator is able to generate another perspective on this information through the use of network analysis, which allows unforeseen connections to emerge. These connections can provide critical insight into their impact on an event.

A network analysis is an organized approach to understanding the impact of information that defines an alleged crime. In practice, the process may be tedious at times, but it is simple in methodology. The utility of network analysis is found in the ability to understand the interdependency of information that is defined through connections between individuals, physical items, locations, and organizations. Two goals are achieved by constructing a network chart: the visualization of information from the perspective of a network and a critical understanding of how facets of information impact connected facets of information. Simply stated, a network analysis allows a criminal defense investigator to uncover the overall impact of the relationship between information that may be elusive when the same information is digested in a narrative format.

Constructing a Network Chart

The process of performing a network analysis is straightforward. Initially, a known point is used as the starting point, generally, the alleged crime scene. From this point, the network is built outward. For example, all known physical evidence is connected to the crime scene and and to individuals. The goal is to illustrate known connections between individuals, physical items, locations, records and organizations.

A network analysis is performed by visualizing a network through a chart. The critical element in generating this chart is utilizing quality information. Nodes are used to represent individuals, physical items, and records. Lines are used to designate connections between the nodes. Two forms of connections should be used: connections that have a high degree of certainty and suspected connections. Locations and organizations should be represented by organizing the nodes on the chart in clusters. The goal is to generate a visual representation of the overall network that existed within an event.

The following should be adhered to when constructing a network chart:

- Confirmed connections should be labeled with a solid line.
- Suspected connections should be labeled with a broken line.
- The type of connection should be identified.
- Nodes of the network should be designated based upon their real life representation through a descriptive label.
- The overall network should be illustrated in a simple format.
- Nodes should be organized based upon their connection to other nodes.
- Locations and organizations should be represented by boxes that contain connected nodes.

Utilizing a Network Chart

A network chart should represent all that is known of an alleged crime from a network perspective. As more information emerges on the alleged crime, the network chart should be continually updated. The chart can be used to understand known information and assess the possibility of elusive information. Beyond gaining an understanding of the networked information, assessing the chart for unknown information is considerably useful. Once the network chart has been generated, anticipated and possible connections should be considered. If these connections are not illustrated on the chart, they could represent a gap in information, which would require continued collection efforts. Anticipated and possible connections on a chart will vary from alleged crime to alleged crime. This variation requires the criminal defense investigator to utilize experience and knowledge of the local area where the crime allegedly occurred in their assessment. Generally, the absence of a connection between any nodes should always be considered on the basis of whether a connection should exist and why the connection is not present.

The following are general areas of consideration when completing an assessment of anticipated and possible connections:

- Unknown connection between individuals
- Unknown connection between individuals and a location
- Unknown connection between individuals and physical evidence
- Unknown connection between individuals and organizations
- Unknown connection between individuals and records
- Unknown connection between physical evidence and a location

Network Analysis Computer Software

The availability of computer software has only increased the tendency to make an otherwise simple process in to a complex one; it causes more confusion than actionable utility. Although computer software exists to generate a network visualization, the author recommends avoiding these forms of software, except in limited applications. Pen and paper typically produce the best results, followed by the use of some form of graphical illustration software to generate a clean visual representation of the network. The detailed knowledge acquired through the tedious assembly of a network cannot be gained through the use of computer software.

Network Analysis Reporting

The network chart is a powerful communication tool. The network chart should be provided to the attorney. In some complex cases, several network charts may be utilized. The use of several charts is typical in cases where specific subnetworks need to be highlighted. In any case, the attorney should only be given the final network chart to prevent any information errors due to the chart's evolution throughout the criminal defense investigation.

Part 3

Chapter 14

Hypothesis Generation

A criminal defense investigator's primary goal is to find evidence of innocence. The second goal is to test the credibility of incriminating evidence. Typically a straightforward approach is utilized while accomplishing these two goals. Simply stated, ideas are formulated on how evidence could be found to meet both goals. The formulation of the an "idea," or hypothesis, is the key factor in this process. Most commonly used when applying the scientific method, hypotheses among criminal defense investigators are largely misunderstood and are underrepresented in a criminal defense investigator's work product. Traditionally, utilizing a hypothesis has not been a mainstream practice of criminal defense investigators or criminal investigators. Instead, investigators largely rely on criminal theories. However, overly generic criminal theories provide little to any utility in reconstructing a historical event. In comparison, an array of hypotheses provide considerable utility during the search for evidence.

The use of hypotheses is commonly misunderstood among criminal defense investigators. Generally, generating and testing hypotheses is viewed as having no utility. This is mainly due to associations of hypotheses with the traditional scientific research. In simple terms, a hypothesis is developed, and an experiment is constructed to test the hypotheses. The testing stage may appear to have little application during criminal defense investigations. However, this is simply not the case. Can a criminal defense investigator formulate a hypothesis then test the hypothesis in the same manner as a scientist? In simple terms, no; this is not possible in the environment encountered by the criminal defense investigator. The criminal defense investigator is unable to construct a precise testing method to determine the validity of a hypothesis in the same way as a practitioner of the hard sciences can. What a criminal defense investigator can do is utilize an array of hypotheses as an instrument during the search for evidence. This is the same process used in the scientific method but breaks from the traditional need to use precise testing to prove or disprove a specific hypothesis.

Utilizing an Array of Hypotheses

Hypotheses are generated on a compounding scale. However, most, if not all, cannot be tested using the traditional application of the scientific method. Reconstructing and testing a historical event is nearly impossible. Only small aspects of the event can be tested with repeatable precision. For example, can a bullet travel along a given trajectory? This question can be answered by formulating a hypothesis and then testing the hypothesis through several known tests. Although the answering this question sheds some light on the historical event under investigation, it will not shed light on the other aspects of the event. Simply stated, many aspects of a historical event cannot be tested and proven in the traditional senses of science. Many would-be investigators attempt to utilize the traditional scientific method with a false senses of certainty. They take a limited view of the subject event based upon the only facet of the event that is testable. The focus should be more on hypnosis generation and less on traditional precision testing.

The endeavor of criminal defense investigators, or any individual attempting to reconstruct a historical event, has one overriding theme: every segment of information, no matter the form, testimony or physical, is evidence. Some evidence has absolutely nothing to do with the subject event. Other evidence has everything to do with the event. The key is distinguishing between relevant and irrelevant evidence.

A hypothesis is the only instrument available to define the utility of evidence. Relevance is the foundation of determining the utility of any evidence in reconstructing a historical event. However, the process of determining relevance is multifaceted and achieved through the use of not just one hypothesis, but an array of hypotheses examined concurrently. The relevance of evidence can only be determined by comparing hypotheses. Simply stated, under close examination, evidence can support more than one hypothesis. By examining an array of hypotheses, an investigator can understand how specific evidence supports or challenges those various hypotheses. As a result, the evidence's utility can be determined.

A hypothesis is an instrument of inquiry. How does a criminal defense investigator know where to find evidence? This is a pressing question throughout any investigation. The tendency, unfortunately, is largely to follow the already established criminal theory of law enforcement, which typically entails exploring only one hypothesis through lead generation. Questions are posed to explore whether the State's evidence really supports the alleged criminal conduct of the defendant. As a result, the criminal defense investigation is narrowed into a limited view of evidence and the identification of new evidence. When an array of hypotheses is utilized by the criminal defense investigator, the resulting search for new evidence is broadened. Simply stated, without the aid of a hypothesis, the possibility of evidence existing to support the subject hypothesis will not be explored. Thus, an array of hypotheses is utilized to force the criminal defense investigator to search for evidence that would be considered nonexistent in the shadow of a single hypothesis.

Hypotheses are the engine that generates the identification of evidence. What about the process of testing each hypothesis? This is the aspect of hypotheses that is typically misunderstood by criminal defense investigators. The search for and identification of evidence is the initial stage of testing a hypothesis. The testing of hypotheses is concluded by comparing of how each facet of evidence supports each hypothesis. In the criminal defense investigator's investigative environment, hypothesis testing is the process of identifying evidence in the shadow of each hypothesis and determining how each piece of evidence impacts all hypotheses. Specific structured analysis techniques are utilized in testing hypotheses. The key is not just accessing one hypothesis but rather an array of hypotheses.

Generating Hypothesis

A general discussion about hypothesis generation can be the abstract work of focus groups, brainstorming strategies, and other creative process at the individual and group level. From the perspective of a criminal defense investigator, specific core concepts need to be addressed that are normally not possible in discussions on the subject. Simply stated, alleged crimes have core themes that allow a focused approach to hypothesis generation.

Although every alleged crime is a unique event in history, the following core possibilities exist in every alleged criminal act:

- The defendant committed the crime.
- The defendant and another person(s) committed the crime.
- An unknown person(s) committed the crime.
- A known person(s) committed the crime.
- A known person(s) and an unknown person(s) committed the crime.
- The accused was not physically capable of committing the crime.
- The accused did not have the necessary resources to commit the crime.
- The accused was not mentally capable of committing the crime.
- The alleged crime was an accident.
- The alleged crime was a conspiracy of the alleged victim(s) or another person(s).

Although the above core possibilities are generalized, an array of hypotheses can be generated based upon these core possibilities. There is no one right why of generating a hypothesis. Essentially, the process is a matter of brainstorming ideas that are written as statements. However, the above core possibilities act as a springboard during this brainstorming process. Each core possibility can be utilized to generate an array of hypotheses. For example, the core possibility that "a known person committed the crime" can be utilized by making an explicit hypothesis about each known witness of the alleged crime. In simple terms, each witness is tested as a possible perpetrator of the crime. In turn, an array of hypotheses is generated based upon this core possibility. A similar approach is taken with each core possibility.

The key to hypothesis generation is to reach beyond the plausible. No matter how unlikely a specific hypothesis is, the hypotheses should still be considered. This is a critical concept in hypothesis generation. In general, if a hypothesis is not considered, there is no possibility of uncovering supporting evidence. As a result, the process of hypothesis generation should be a viewed completely as a theoretical exercise to prevent bias in the face of known information. If not, then information known to the criminal defense investigator can cause a group of hypotheses to be considered implausible without any attempt to validate them through investigation. Therefore, a complete array of hypotheses should be generated based upon all core possibilities.

While brainstorming possible hypotheses, each hypothesis should not be considered in isolation, but as part of a pair of competing hypothesis. The goal is to establish a balanced approach of testing hypotheses. For example, if the core possibility that "the accused was not physically capable of committing the crime" is being considered than for every hypothesis generated, a second, opposing hypothesis should be generated. The following is an example of polar opposite hypotheses:

The defendant is physically capable of committing the alleged crime.

The defendant is not physically capable of committing the alleged crime.

Generating hypotheses in pairs forces the criminal defense investigator to explore possibilities in a balanced and holistic approach. Simply stated, if a coin was being examined to check if it is counterfeit, would the examiner not look at both sides of the coin? If the examiner only examined one side, would not the examiner's judgement be limited to a confidence level of only 50%? If, however, the examiner utilized both sides of the coin during the examination, would not a higher degree of confidence be possible than just 50%?

This is a simplistic example, but it illustrates the problematic process of only considering one hypothesis versus considering that and an opposing hypothesis.

A core concern during hypothesis generation is the level of detail that is examined through the hypotheses. Simply stated, should a hypothesis be posed at the level of the person or at the level of the specific action? For example, John Doe killed Jane Doe (person level) or John Doe shot Jane Doe (action level). Answering this question of detail is always problematic and presents a degree of liability in committing an error in judgment. Thus, a systematic framework should be utilized to determine the level of detail required of each hypothesis.

Initially, when generating hypotheses, the detail level should be set at the person level. Every known person and the possibility of unknown persons should be included in the threshold of the hypothesis array. This is from the high-level diagnostic view of the alleged crime. The key is that any alleged crime is a holistic event. However, as information emerges during the investigation, a lower level of detail at the action level should be explored through an additional hypothesis array. This utilization of hypotheses at the action level should be applied to critical segments of evidence. For example, could a witness travel a known distance through an alleged means of travel? In examining this form of critical evidence, a pair of polar opposite hypotheses should be used to explore each possibility for the witness's means of travel. Thus, the evidence's credibility and the overall interpretation will be determined.

Core evidence is a critical concept in examining the action level through a hypothesis array. The concept of core evidence is expressed in the Criminal Activity Equation:

$$\textit{Criminal Activity = Intent + Opportunity + Ability}$$

Intent, opportunity, and ability can be represented in a wide array of evidence forms, from physical evidence to witness testimony; the possibilities are endless. Typically, this evidence will emerge as the core evidence that defines the alleged crime, for example, the timeframe during which the crime allegedly occurred, the weapon and method used during an alleged assault, or entry and exit into and from a building during a burglary. All of these examples are directly tied to the Criminal Activity Equation and in a real world investigation should be included within the hypothesis array at the action level.

Simply generating a hypothesis array is not adequate to meet the needs of a criminal defense investigation. The array must be developed and utilized through structured analysis to have any real actionable utility. This book present two methods for utilizing hypotheses, probable event analysis and the analysis of competing hypotheses.

Chapter 15

Probable Event Analysis

The methods used to interpret evidence vary from investigator to investigator. Typically, an intuitive approach is used to interpret evidence, and the approach is not easily communicated from one investigator to the next. The only exception is the use of forensic evidence, which is scientifically based and limited in evidence interpretation. As a result, investigators are faced with abstract information derived from human observations and crime scene dynamics that must be woven together to generate an understanding of what may have occurred. The interpretation of evidence is currently a considerable weakness within the overall endeavor of criminal investigation. Evidence interpretation is not just a matter of understanding the meaning of evidence but also the identification of evidence. Understanding and identifying evidence are intertwined. Criminal defense investigation is riddled with this same weakness. A method founded in abductive reasoning is needed to eliminate the weakness of evidence interpretation as it relates to an alleged crime.

Methods of collecting evidence and determining where evidence may be found has been well defined in criminal investigations. However, the interpretation of evidence has been ill defined among law enforcement practitioners. Based upon the author's own training, formal education, and experience as a working police officer, the interpretation of evidence by law enforcement officers is based upon dogmatic perceptions driven by egocentric bias. The opposing endeavor of criminal defense investigation is also riddled with bias, considering the foundation training of many criminal defense investigators is obtained in law enforcement or other bias-riddled professions. As a result, criminal investigations, by law enforcement or defense investigators, are impacted by the investigators' own perceptions of evidence. The identification and interpretation of evidence related to an alleged crime is a subjective endeavor.

Two issues exist in relation to criminal evidence: the issue of measurement and the issue of credibility. Measurement is the examination of the diagnostic value of one piece of evidence in comparison to other evidence.[33] On the other hand, credibility is the examination of the quality of specific evidence in respect of subterfuge or misconceptions. The most common themes of evidence credibility are misconceived comprehension and evidence trustworthiness. This is evident during a criminal trial, as the two opposing sides make arguments. These two themes can be generated by intentional or unintentional acts.

In theory, evidence of a crime is subjective, and is collected and interpreted based upon an investigator's assumptions and investigative theory. In the end, the assumed evidence is further interpreted through logical arguments made by the prosecutor and defense attorney. This process of theory, assumption, collection, and interpretation starts with one single inquiry. An example is "Who killed Jane Doe?" In the same token, academic and professional researchers start a research endeavor with a single line of inquiry known as a research question. In essence, investigation and research may be considered the same form of inquiry. The only difference is the methods of inquiry used.

Based on the author's own law enforcement experience, criminal investigations are based on intuitive reasoning, with some exceptions. In theory, criminal investigators employ logical deductive reasoning coupled with their expert opinion, in some cases. The expert opinion is usually derived from consultation with forensic scientists or the investigator's own training and professional experience. This is contrary to the conduct of the working professionals

_____

[33] Pennington, Jeremy Lee. "Measuring Evidence During Criminal Defense Investigations Through Analysis of Competing Hypotheses (ACH)." SSRN Journal (December 11, 2012).

who actually pursue criminal investigations. In reality, criminal investigations can best be described as a fisherman casting a net. When the net is pulled in, fish caught in it is the prime suspect. From this point forward, all efforts are focused on this fish until a presumed logical argument is generated supporting the right to suspect the fish. This is the point where "evidence" truly becomes a phenomenon of perception.

Evidence as a phenomenon of perception derives from a wide array of causes, but in the case of criminal investigations, the overwhelming need is to bring closure. Typically, the vehicle for closure is the arrest and successful prosecution of a person. The byproduct of this need for closure is proclaiming the first fish is the correct one. In many cases, the guilt of the first fish is nothing more than a theory, but information uncovered throughout the investigation is subsequently judged based upon this theory. Information perceived to support the theory is deemed to be evidence, and all other information is rejected. This phenomenon is known as a "satisficing strategy."[34] A satisficing criminal investigation is one that is closed through an arrest and prosecution on the basis of one criminal theory.

From a criminal defense investigator's perspective, evidence as a phenomenon of perception is a real and dangerous reality. In practice, a criminal defense investigator's goal is to discredit existing evidence of guilt and provide new evidence to support an alternative theory.

Probable event analysis (PEA) is a structured analysis technique specifically used during criminal defense investigations. PEA is not meant to be used alone but as one of many possible instruments used in criminal defense. Most notably, PEA is an instrument of considerable utility in judging the credibility of evidence and discovering unknown evidence in a field investigation. The use of PEA is meant to be coupled with the method known as the analysis of competing hypotheses (ACH).

---

[34] Heuer, Richards J. Psychology of Intelligence Analysis. Center for the Study of Intelligence, 1999., p 96

PEA produces logical arguments to discredit proposed evidence, assist the investigator in uncovering otherwise unseen evidence, and, most critically, enhance the development of alternate theories in relation to specific evidence at the "action level" versus the "person level." PEA forces the criminal defense investigator to shift from the use of deductive perception to abductive perception. This provides a bridge from one criminal theory approach to an array of criminal theories.

Theoretical Lens of PEA

Through the theoretical lens of PEA, all events and specific items of evidence are viewed in opposing sets. In simple terms, no event or evidence supports a single theory or hypothesis but rather supports at least two opposing hypotheses. This theoretical lens is used to view the incident under inquiry through all segments of information associated with the incident. The overall incident is not considered as a whole, but the individual facets of the incident are assessed alone at the "action level." Thus, two opposing hypotheses are proposed for every single segment of information.

The opposing hypotheses approach of PEA allows an investigator to assess an array of possibilities regarding what the evidence may represent. The utility of PEA is in its comprehensive approach to assessing the significance of evidence. This assessment is completed at the lowest level possible, the "action level." For example, during a murder investigation, a single footprint is found in soft soil in the immediate area of the victim's body. What does this footprint represent? Is it the murderer's footstep? This possibly could lead to the identification of the murder, or at least, this is the view traditionally taken. On the other hand, is the footprint simply a footprint from an unrelated event? One hypothesis is used to examine the possibility that the footprint represents the footstep of the murderer, while the opposing hypothesis allows for another interpretation of the same evidence. What evidence exists to support one hypothesis versus another? Most evidence will support more than one hypothesis; however, the goal is to determine which evidence only supports one hypothesis. This evidence is core evidence.

The significance of some evidence, after careful consideration, has little to no value in determining historical events. Essentially, the evidence landscape presents a wide array of information for determining the historical events of an alleged crime. Many individual segments of information hold no utility in making an intelligent assessment of an historical event. The wide array of information available acts as a fog over the investigation, creating confusion. The key is determining which specific segments of information are connected to the alleged crime as evidence, known as critical evidence, and which segments represent irrelevant events in history.

In application, PEA is meant as an instrument of comparison. A single segment of information is assessed based upon the possibility that the information represents two opposing alternative views. In simple terms, a single segment of information is taken under consideration, and two possible explanations are explored. For example, a ball falls from the sky. Did the ball fall from outer space? Was the ball kicked from an adjacent area? Without any information other than the ball fell from the sky, both questions can be found to be true. However, more information is needed to fully assess both questions. The key is viewing each question as a scenario and then attempting to support each theoretical scenario with evidence. Was there a child in an adjacent area playing with a ball? Was a ball in orbit around the Earth? What other possible scenarios can be posed as questions and then answered through field investigation? The overall goal of PEA is sorting information through a comparative strategy of investigation.

In terms of criminal defense investigation, the comparative strategy should be highlighted by opposing, positive-negative perspectives. For every segment of information, one positive scenario, expressed through a hypothesis, and one negative scenario should be generated. In many cases, the negative scenario will already be proposed by law enforcement. In turn, the criminal defense investigator must generate an opposing alternative "positive" scenario. A positive scenario represents the innocence of the defendant or a scenario of an unrelated alternative event. However, when there are common items of physical evidence and common occurrences, the criminal defense investigator should assess multiple alternative positive scenarios.

The PEA is applied through the following steps:

1. Identify the information segment.

2. Determine the opposing positive-negative scenarios that the information segment possibly represents.

3. Search for information to support each positive and negative scenario.

4. Reassess to determine if any additional positive alternative scenarios exist.

5. Evaluate any information in support of opposing positive-negative scenarios.

    A. If information exists supporting the positive and negative scenario, the information is accepted as neutral evidence.

    B. If information exists supporting the positive scenario but not the negative scenario, the information is accepted as evidence of innocence.

    C. If information exists supporting the negative scenario but not the positive scenario, the information is accepted as evidence of guilt.

    D. If no information exists supporting the positive or negative scenario, the information is rejected as unrelated information.

The above five-step process should be repeated with every segment of information encountered by the criminal defense investigator. With each facet of information, two opposing scenarios are proposed as hypotheses: one negative and one positive. Then, additional information is searched for to support both hypotheses. Once this information is uncovered or confirmed to not exist, the segment of information under examination is evaluated based upon four possible outcomes.

If information exists supporting the positive and negative scenarios, the information is accepted as neutral evidence.

The following is an example of an evaluation leading to the above result: During a murder investigation, a single footprint is found in soft soil in the immediate area of the victim's body.

Negative hypothesis: The defendant's shoes match the footprint found at the crime scene.

Positive hypothesis: The defendant's shoes are issued by the largest area employer.

Information uncovered: The defendant owns a matching pair of shoes that were issued by the largest employer in the city. The number of employees issued identical shoes is approximately 3,256.

If information exists supporting the positive scenario but not the negative scenario, the information is accepted as evidence of innocence.

The following is an example of an evaluation leading to the above result: During a murder investigation, a single footprint is found in soft soil in the immediate area of the victim's body.

Negative hypothesis: The defendant's shoes match the footprint found at the crime scene.

Positive hypothesis: The defendant's shoes are issued by the largest area employer.

Information uncovered: The defendant does not own a matching pair of shoes that were issued by the largest employer in the city. The number of employees issued identical shoes is approximately 3,256.

If information exists supporting the negative scenario but not the positive scenario, the information is accepted as evidence of guilt.

The following is an example of an evaluation leading to the above result: During a murder investigation, a single footprint is found in soft soil in the immediate area of the victim's body.

Negative hypothesis: The defendant's shoes match the footprint found at the crime scene.

Positive hypothesis: The defendant's shoes are issued by the largest area employer.

Information uncovered: The defendant does own a matching pair of shoes. The largest employer in the city does not issue shoes to any employees.

If no information exists supporting the positive or negative scenario, the information is rejected as unrelated information.

The following is an example of an evaluation leading to the above result: During a murder investigation, a single footprint is found in soft soil in the immediate area of the victim's body.

Negative hypothesis: The defendant's shoes match the footprint found at the crime scene.

Positive hypothesis: The defendant's shoes are issued by the largest area employer.

Information uncovered: The defendant does not own a matching pair of shoes. The largest employer in the city does not issue shoes to any employees.

Understanding PEA in application is directly dependent on understating the concept of generating opposing hypotheses. The above example is overly simplistic and overly broad. However, it demonstrates how information is evaluated through PEA. In application, overly broad hypotheses would not be generated, for example, the idea of the defendant's shoe being issued by a large area employer. This example was only used to clearly communicate the concept of information evaluation.

The end goal of PEA is to enable the criminal defense investigator's evaluation of information based upon the information's supporting information. Simply stated, is the information really evidence when considering its context from an alternative perspective? However, PEA is utilized in a field based environment. Therefore, the process is haphazard and should not be the primary instrument of diagnostic analysis during an investigation. Why even utilize the method considering the possibility of errors? Field operations allow the criminal defense investigator's immersion in the environment where the crime allegedly occurred. This allows the criminal defense investigator to make considerations that are not adequately possible when outside of the environment. This environmental immersion provides insight, but it can also limit the criminal defense investigator's broader view. Thus, PEA is not utilized as a primary diagnostic instrument but rather as a diagnostic aid during collection operations.

Chapter 16

Analysis of Competing Hypotheses

Matters of criminal defense are posed with one critical issue, which has two distinct adversarial views. These two competing views can be framed as hypotheses. Each side presents and argues evidence to support a proposed hypothesis. The evidence presented, along with skilled arguments supporting each hypotheses, is decided upon by the judiciary. In some cases, one hypothesis gains considerable weight over the opposing hypothesis, and the opposing side succumbs to the demands of the prevailing hypothesis's architect. This, in turn, leads to a settlement or plea bargain. The similarities of this context to the historical use of the analysis of competing hypotheses (ACH) method is undeniable.

ACH has been used by professional intelligence analysts since the 1970s. Generally, this method is used to make difficult probability judgments involving many different alternative hypotheses. In short, the goal is to find and select the hypothesis most likely to become true during predictive research. ACH is considered by some as the most robust form of qualitative analysis available. An examination of ACH reveals its utility in the measurement, comparison, and diagnostic exploration of criminal evidence.

Criminal defense investigators are tasked with supporting criminal defense attorneys. The type of support varies between different investigator-attorney relationships. However, at the foundation, criminal defense investigators have the task of sorting and measuring the impact of information. This information is deconstructed and organized to create a coherent image of the alleged crime, allowing the defense attorney to competently argue a defense. Critical aspects of information can be easily overlooked while sifting for critical facts.

The criminal defense investigator is responsible for three critical tasks involving information: reviewing the information presented by the prosecution team, uncovering new information that is either denied or unknown by the prosecution, and deconstructing and measuring all information for its impact on the overall defense strategy. The resulting analysis is communicated to and interpreted by the defense attorney. However, there is a high risk of error during the process. The criminal defense investigator or attorney could easily miss a pivotal fact or fail to search for specific evidence due to bias. Historically, this process has been completed through intuitive reasoning, which is error prone. An investigator can miss pivotal information based on the sheer volume of information or fail to recognize a critical fact. ACH presents the opportunity to alleviate the errors historically encountered by investigators.

ACH in Theory, Method, and Practice

ACH was originally meant for predictive research on an international scale, specifically dealing with issues of U.S. national security. Ideally, this method is used to evaluate controversial issues that are placed under considerable scrutiny.[35] Several procedural methods are built into the ACH method that support national security goals. The use of an array of hypotheses represents several plausible future events. Thus, ACH is a method of selecting the right hypothesis or event in the face of abstract information.

ACH was created by Heuer (1999).[36] In ACH, a hypothesis is defined as a "potential explanation or conclusion," which is examined by collecting evidence and formulating

---

[35] Red Team Handbook. 5th ed. University of Foreign Military and Cultural Studies, 2011. http://usacac.army.mil/cac2/UFMCS/repository/RT_Handbook_v5_Apr11.pdf., p. 158

[36] Heuer, Richards J. Psychology of Intelligence Analysis. Center for the Study of Intelligence, 1999., p. 95

174

arguments.[37] The **ACH** method requires the explicit identification of all plausible alternative hypotheses and lays them in competition for favor by the practicing analyst while minimizing cognitive limitations.[38] This method breaks from the traditional approach of qualitative intuitive reasoning.

The ACH method, as described by Heuer, (1999) is presented below for clarity:

1. *Identify the possible hypotheses to be considered. Use a group of analysts with different perspectives to brainstorm the possibilities.*

2. *Make a list of significant evidence and arguments for and against each hypothesis.*

3. *Prepare a matrix with hypotheses across the top and evidence down the side. Analyze the "diagnosticity" of the evidence and arguments—that is, identify which items are most helpful in judging the relative likelihood of the hypotheses.*

4. *Refine the matrix. Reconsider the hypotheses and delete evidence and arguments that have no diagnostic value.*

5. *Draw tentative conclusions about the relative likelihood of each hypothesis. Proceed by trying to disprove the hypotheses rather than prove them.*

6. *Analyze how sensitive your conclusions are to a few critical items of evidence. Consider the consequence for your analysis if that evidence were wrong, misleading, or subject to different interpretation.*

7. *Report conclusions. Discuss the relative likelihood of all the hypotheses, not just the most likely one.*

8. *Identify milestones for future observation that may indicate events are taking a different course than expected.[39]*

ACH allows the intelligence analyst to overcome the inherent limitations of human memory. The process of generating a matrix of hypotheses and evidence allows the analyst to evaluate information in a systematic process. Otherwise, the endeavor would overload an

---

[37] Ibid.

[38] Ibid

[39] Ibid, p. 97

analyst with information.[40] ACH is a model for evaluating complex problems.[41] The ACH process acts as a vehicle for applying the scientific method to complex qualitative problems.[42] However, the limitations of predictive analysis are that a hypothesis cannot be tested using the application of the scientific method; this is the same during criminal defense investigations.[43] Thus, ACH stands as the most approximate contemporary approach to evaluating qualitative data without testing hypotheses.

ACH is a method that is intended to overcome the analyst's cognitive limitations. Analysts intuitively select their preferred hypothesis.[44] In short, this occurs when the analyst specifically selects evidence supporting their favored hypothesis and discounting any non-supporting evidence. This phenomenon has been termed "satisficing," or selective perception.[45] During ACH, the analyst is attempting to disprove each hypothesis as enumerated in the fifth step of the ACH method.[46] Thus, the analyst is positioned to examine an array of hypotheses rather than focus solely on one hypothesis.

Engaging an array of hypotheses is critical. The most devastating aspect of engaging a single hypothesis is the overwhelming odds that an incorrect hypothesis is being advanced. The general idea is to initially engage a large array of hypotheses. However, the structured

---

[40] Heuer, Richards J. "Chapter 16 Computer-Aided Analysis of Competing Hypotheses." In Analyzing Intelligence: Origins, Obstacles, and Innovations, edited by Roger Z. George and James B. Bruce. Washington, D.C.: Georgetown University Press, 2008., p. 253

[41] Ibid.

[42] Ibid.

[43] Ibid.

[44] Ibid., p. 105

[45] Ibid., p. 44

[46] Ibid.

analysis of competing hypotheses (SACH), a version of ACH, uses different approach.[47] SACH uses what is termed a "drill-down" effect.[48] In short, the analysis begins by utilizing only two different hypotheses in the early stages. After finding one hypothesis true, additional research questions are asked to generate more hypotheses. The argument for using SACH versus ACH is the prevention of cognitive bias. ACH was advanced with the same rationale. To date, these two opposing methods are used at the analyst's discretion. Nevertheless, the simple reality is that the use of only two hypotheses does not lead to the diagnosticity of evidence. The lack of a hypothesis array limits the search for evidence during analysis. The primary strength of ACH is its diagnostic value.

Diagnostic value can be framed as the evidence's value across all hypotheses. Diagnostic value is not the support of all hypotheses, but the explicit support of one select hypothesis.[49] Heuer (1999) asserts that a common experience during the use of ACH is an analyst finding favored evidence that supports their preferred hypothesis as well as several other hypotheses. In turn, the evidence holds no diagnostic value. Heuer (1999) determined that identified diagnostic evidence should drive judgments. Thus, in theory, judgments made through ACH are highly objective.

The objectivity of ACH is dependent on the hypothesis array. Step one of the ACH method requires the identification of all possible hypotheses for consideration. The hypothesis array is directly tied to the ability to find and evaluate all available evidence. If a critical hypothesis remains unavailable during analysis, then the diagnostic value of specific evidence's will remain undiscovered. Thus, hypothesis generation is a critical step.

---

[47] Wheaton, Kristan J., Mercyhurst College, and Diane E. Chido. "Structured Analysis of Competing Hypotheses." Competitive Intelligence Magazine 9, no. November-December (2006): 1–4. http://www.mcmanis-monsalve.com/files/publications/intelligence-methodology-1-07-chido.pdf., p. 14

[48] Ibid.

[49] Ibid., p. 102

ACH in Criminal Defense

Criminal litigation is a prime environment for the application of ACH. It is human nature to seek a smoking gun when placing blame. However, an environment composed of strict qualitative information is normally not acquainted with a trenchant piece of evidence. In some cases, such evidence may not be available, and in other cases the relationship may not be readily apparent. In the best of cases, ACH is a means to uncover an unseen smoking gun in criminal litigation.

Human cognitive limitations increase with the complexity of an investigation. Cognitive limitations are normally not an issue in simple investigations that include a small number of variables. However, as investigative variables increase, the limitations of human cognition have a compounding effect. In short, humans simply are unable to organize, measure, and effectively evaluate a large number of variables.

Figure 8.1 - ACH Example Matrix

Hypothesis #1 (H1) – The defendant committed the murder.

Hypothesis #2 (H2) – committed the murder.

	H1	H2
Defendant had motive to murder the victim	+	-
Defendant was alone with the victim (Late returning to the meeting)	+	-
Seven people had access to the victim	+	+
The victim's body (350 pounds) was lifted five feet from the ground	-	+

A prime example of this cognitive limitation is a criminal defense scenario involving a group of suspects. An investigating law enforcement agency arrests one suspect based on an admission during the interrogation of the defendant. There is a meeting that includes seven suspects and the victim. During a brief break from the meeting, lasting no longer then fifteen minutes, all individuals exit into a long corridor with bathrooms, vending areas, and storage areas. Upon returning to the meeting, the victim is unaccounted for, and one other individual is also missing, the defendant. The meeting reconvenes. Fifteen minutes later, the defendant returns to the meeting stating that he became sick in the restroom. The victim never returns.

Two days later, law enforcement is contacted by the victim's family. Six days later, the victim's body is found in a storage area adjacent to the meeting room in a cabinet that required the murderer to lift the victim five feet off the ground. The victim is described, by law enforcement officers, as six-feet tall weighing three hundred and fifty pounds. The resulting investigation determined the occupancy of the building was limited to the meeting attendees. The defendant and the victim had a public disagreement two days prior to the incident, and a long, well-known adversarial relationship. Figure 8.1 is an example of how this information would be used within an ACH matrix.

Considering the victim's known relationship with the defendant, we assume the defendant had a motive to murder the victim. This conclusion is represented by a "+" mark under hypothesis H1. In the same token, the defendant and victim had the opportunity to be alone prior to the murder, which is signified by an additional "+" mark under H1. The victim was in contact with seven people preceding the murder. Because the defendant is one of the seven people, both H1 and H2 receive a "+" mark. Lastly, the victim's body weighs three hundred and fifty pounds. An average person would feasibly be unable to lift the victim's body five feet from the ground. Thus, H1 receives a "-" mark, and H2 receives a "+" mark.

Examining the matrix reveals four key points. Three of these key points are arbitrary: one, the defendant, based on the matrix, had access to the victim, two, the meeting group as a whole had access to the victim, and three, the defendant is assumed to have a motive. The primary key point that holds diagnostic value is the victim's body weight and the placement of the body. This diagnostic value should be the driving factor of the investigation. With this diagnostic value, a Criminal defense investigator only needs to prove the defendant is unable to physically lift the victim's body five feet off the ground, either through natural means or through some form of assistance.

Why does the body weight hold diagnostic value and the remaining evidence does not? A critical examination of the matrix shows that the body weight does not support the H1 hypotheses. This is critical in understanding how to utilize ACH during a criminal defense investigation. Yes, H1 is supported by other evidence but not by the issue of body weight. Why does the body weight become so critical during our evaluation? In short, the body weight supports a single hypothesis.

Figure 8.2 - ACH Example Matrix

Hypothesis #1 (H1) – The defendant committed the murder.

Hypothesis #2 (H2) – An unknown person(s) committed the murder.

	H1	H2
Defendant had motive to murder the victim	+	-
Defendant was alone with the victim (Late returning to the meeting)	+	-
The victim's body (350 pounds) was lifted five feet from the ground	-	+

The diagnostic value of the body weight becomes more apparent in Figure 8.2, where it becomes clearer that it supports only one hypothesis: H2. Moreover, there is no other evidence supporting this same hypothesis. Yes, the remaining evidence does support H1. However, the issue of body weight only supports H2. Why does this evidence not support H1? More importantly, why is this lack of support for H1 significant? Simply stated, H1 is disproved by the existence of the body weight issue. In the same token, H2 is disproved by the existence of evidence that only supports H1. The significance of the body weight evidence in supporting one hypotheses drives the investigator to reconsider the favored hypothesis and its underlying supporting evidence.

In practice, the diagnostic value of the body weight would force the criminal defense investigator to consider additional hypotheses and search for evidence to support these hypotheses. In the process, the investigator would exhaust all possible hypotheses until only one remains. It is important to note that ACH is not about declaring a winner but considering possibilities. ACH is meant to determine the likelihood of each hypothesis.

This example is meant to demonstrate the application of ACH in criminal defense investigations. An array of hypotheses can be evaluated based on available evidence. Specific evidence can be measured based on "diagnosticity." The critical aspect of ACH is that evidence can be evaluated, using a matrix, across a wide spectrum of possible hypotheses. ACH can allow the criminal defense investigator to determine what is and what is not known with a given degree of certainty. In turn, ACH holds considerable utility for criminal defense investigator through the measurement, comparison, and diagnostic exploration of criminal evidence.

Utilizing ACH

ACH should be viewed as a rallying point during any investigation. Before ACH is utilized, a good footing should already be in place. Simply stated, the criminal defense investigator should have already processed the discovery file using information quality checks, completed the required collection operations, and completed the analytical techniques presented earlier in this book.

For clarity each step of ACH is examined in detail from the perspective of a criminal defense investigator:

1. Identify the possible hypotheses to be considered. Use a group of analysts with different perspectives to brainstorm the possibilities.

The previously developed hypothesis array is utilized during this step. However, hypothesis generation should be a continuous process. This can include obtaining additional perspectives from peer investigators, but in many cases this may not be possible.

2. Make a list of significant evidence and arguments for and against each hypothesis.

During this step, all investigative data and analytical products should be considered for inclusion. The criminal defense investigator must ensure any information utilized has been fully vetted through an information quality check. This step also includes "arguments." From the perspective of a criminal defense investigation, "arguments" include any known analytical judgements made by the State and any interpretation of the evidence made by the criminal defense investigator.

3. Prepare a matrix with hypotheses across the top and evidence down the side. Analyze the "diagnosticity" of the evidence and arguments—that is, identify which items are most helpful in judging the relative likelihood of the hypotheses.

In this step, hypotheses are plotted across the top of the matrix. Then, each facet of information is considered for inclusion on the matrix. This can be a haphazard process in the hands of an unskilled investigator. Generally, an investigator with limited experience should include all information and then consider the "diagnosticity" of each piece of evidence. However, an experienced investigator can make these judgments with a high degree of certainty without plotting all information. As a rule, the Criminal Activity Equation should be the foundation when making these considerations:

$$\textit{Criminal Activity = Intent + Opportunity + Ability}$$

The following aspects of evidence should be considered when plotting evidence:

- The chronology of events that define the alleged crime
- The credibility of each piece of evidence
- The existence of absent evidence

4. Refine the matrix. Reconsider the hypotheses and delete evidence and arguments that have no diagnostic value.

In this step, hypotheses and evidence holding no diagnostic value are eliminated. Simply stated, information is reduced from a large to a consumable scale. In practice, all evidence supporting a large number of hypotheses should be eliminated.

5. Draw tentative conclusions about the relative likelihood of each hypothesis. Proceed by trying to disprove rather than prove each hypotheses.

In this step, a critical review of each piece of evidence is undertaken. A revised view of each hypothesis is taken, where the focus is on disproving rather than proving each hypothesis. Then, each facet of evidence is assessed to ascertain whether it supports a specific hypothesis. Simply stated, the investigator focuses on why the evidence would not support a specific hypothesis rather than whether the evidence supports the specific hypotheses. This approach to assessing each facet of evidence is key during the ACH process.

6. Analyze how sensitive your conclusions are to a few critical items of evidence. Consider the consequence for your analysis if that evidence were wrong, misleading, or subject to different interpretation.

In this step, critical evidence is assessed. What is considered critical evidence? Again, from the perspective of a criminal defense investigation, this comes back to the Criminal Activity Equation:

Criminal Activity = Intent + Opportunity + Ability

The equation should be the theoretical lens from which all evidence is viewed and assessed. The consideration is made if the analysis is wrong from the perspective of each piece of evidence. The Investigative Evidentiary Equation is the foundation of this this assessment:

Event = Evidence + Silent Evidence - Absent Evidence - Credibility

The Investigative Evidentiary Equation represents a process underlying the ACH. The option exists to rank each piece of evidence based upon its credibility. Instead of simply utilizing a "-" or "+" symbol, evidence supporting a hypotheses can be indicated on a scale of 1 through 10, "1" representing the lowest credibility and "10" representing the high level of credibility. During the more generalized application of ACH, a similar scale can be utilized to indicate the level of support a facet of evidence lends to a specific hypothesis. However, this method is not recommended in a criminal defense setting due to the preferred usage of a credibility variable.

7. Report conclusions. Discuss the relative likelihood of all the hypotheses, not just the most likely one.

In this step, a consideration is made of the prior results. The resulting matrix is viewed from the perspective of an array of possible answers based upon the relative likelihood of each hypothesis. In turn, the resulting conclusion is then incorporated into the ongoing investigation.

8. Identify milestones for future observation that may indicate events are taking a different course than expected.

ACH is utilized in predictive analysis; as a consequence, this step may seem of place during a criminal defense investigation. However, this is not the case. A "milestone" in a criminal defense investigation represents information that could emerge that changes the overall conclusions of the analysis, for example, a codefendant turning State witness, an new witness proving incriminating testimony, or the results of a pending forensic test. Milestones are critical aspects of a criminal defense investigation, not because they require further collection operations but because of the possibility of silent evidence.

Utilizing ACH in The Real World

Implementing ACH during real-life, complex investigations can be an overwhelming task for an investigator. Considering the ACH matrix will be reassessed and reassessed over the lifespan of an investigation, this is an ideal issue to be handled through the use of computer software. A spreadsheet serves this purpose well. The use of spreadsheets allows easy transfer to a written report and overall manipulation of the ACH matrix. There is specific software available for ACH through Palo Alto Research Center. This software has considerable utility and automates the manipulation of the ACH matrix. However, the software does not allow the matrix to be exported into a printable format, which makes generating a report difficult. The software is freely available for download through the following URL:

http://www2.parc.com/istl/projects/ach/ach.html

ACH Reporting

The results of an ACH analysis should be reported to the defense attorney. This serves two purposes in the investigator-attorney relationship. First, the attorney is able to understand the criminal defense investigator's professional opinion of the alleged crime within a format that can be audited. The ability to audit an analysis completed through ACH is one of the reasons the method is utilized during controversial issues. Therefore, the criminal defense investigator must ensure an adequate amount of detail is available on the matrix for this audit to take place. References to original source documents is helpful in this respect. Second, the attorney is able to utilize the ACH matrix when attempting to understand the criminal defense case as a whole and while generating arguments. ACH reporting should occur late in the investigation in order to reflect the utilization of the ACH method throughout the investigation. Simply stated, ACH will be completed several times throughout an investigation of a single alleged crime. The matrix will go through several revisions as new information emerges and additional hypotheses are considered. Only the final ACH matrix should be provide to the attorney to prevent any overlap or errors in information.

Bibliography

Aiken, J.H., and J.C. Murphy. "Dealing with Complex Evidence of Domestic Violence: a Primer for the Civil Bench." Court Review: The Journal of the American Judges Association 39, no. 2 (2002): 141.

Almond, L, L Alison, and L Porter. "An Evaluation and Comparison of Claims Made in Behavioral Investigative Advice Reports Compiled by the National Policing Improvements Agency in the United Kingdom." Journal of Investigative Psychology and Offender Profiling 4, no. 2 (2007): 71–83.

Anand, Ravi. "Proof of the Identification Parade." SSRN Journal (2009).

Ashworth, A. "Four Threats to the Presumption of Innocence'(2006)." International Journal of Evidence and Proof 10 (n.d.): 241.

Bard, Jennifer S. "'Oh Yes, I Remember It Well': Why the Inherent Unreliability of Technology Which Purports to Retrieve Human Memories Makes It Inappropriate for Forensic Use." SSRN Journal (2011).

Bell, Jeannine. "Behind This Mortal Bone: the (in)Effectiveness of Torture." Social Science Research Network (July 23, 2008).

Bell, Jeannine. "One Thousand Shades of Gray: the Effectiveness of Torture." Social Science Research Network (August 15, 2005).

Bhotika, Abhyuday. "Evidentiary Value of First Information Report (FIR)." SSRN Journal (2011).

Blandon-Gitlin, I., K. Sperry, and R. Leo. "Jurors Believe Interrogation Tactics Are Not Likely to Elicit False Confessions: Will Expert Witness Testimony Inform Them Otherwise?." Psychology, Crime & Law 17, no. 3 (2011): 239–260.

Campbell, Erreka. "Ditch the Snitch: Why State and Federal Governments Should Limit the Use and Admissibility of Informant Testimony." SSRN Journal (2011).

Cheikes, Brant A., Mark J. Brown, Leonard Adelman, and Paul E. Lehner. Confirmation Bias in Complex Analyses. Bedford: MITRE Center for Integrated Intelligence Systems, 2004. http://www.mitre.org/work/tech_papers/tech_papers_04/04_0985/04_0985.pdf.

Chesser, Nancy, ed. "Anticipating Rare Events: Can Acts of Terror, Use of Weapons of Mass Destruction or Other High Profile Acts Be Anticipated? a Scientific Perspective on Problems, Pitfalls and Prospective Solutions." Read Team Journal (November 2008): 1–205. http://redteamjournal.com/papers/U_White_Paper-Anticipating_Rare_Events_Nov2008rev.pdf.

Christianson, S.Å., E. Engelberg, and Å. Gustafson. "Recognition of Previous Eyewitness Testimony From an Altered Interrogation Protocol: Potential Effects of Distortions." Psychology, Crime \& Law 13, no. 6 (2007): 583–589.

Ciampolini, A, and P Torroni. "Using Abductive Logic Agents for Modeling the Judicial Evaluation of Criminal Evidence." Applied Artificial Intelligence 18, no. 3-4 (2004): 251–275.

Clermont, K.M., and E. Sherwin. "A Comparative View of Standards of Proof." The American Journal of Comparative Law 50, no. 2 (2002): 243–275.

Convertino, Gregorio, Dorrit Billman, JP Masur, Peter Pirolli, and Jeff Shrager. "Collaborative Intelligence Analysis with CACHE: Bias Reduction and Information Coverage" (n.d.): 1–10. http://cll.stanford.edu/~billman/publications/CSCW06PARCConvertinoBillman.pdf.

Convertino, Gregorio, Dorrit Billman, Peter Pirolli, J. P. Massar, and Jeff Shrager. "The CACHE Study: Group Effects in Computer-Supported Collaborative Analysis." Last modified 2008. Accessed April 22, 2012. http://web.ebscohost.com.ezproxy2.apus.edu/ehost/pdfviewer/pdfviewer?vid=11&hid=21&sid=5d6fc078-d1eb-4a0b-8cb4-3b605a2bbe9e%40sessionmgr14.

Dahl, Leora Catherine, University of Victoria (Canada). Investigating Investigators: How Presentation Order Influences Investigators' Interpretations of Alibi and Bystander Witness Evidence. ProQuest, 2007.

DiGuiseppi, Christine. "Eyewitness Report.Qxd:Layout 3" (June 23, 2009): 1–45. http://www.innocenceproject.org/docs/Eyewitness_ID_Report.pdf.

Duncan, K.A., and J.L. Wilson. "A Multinomial-Dirichlet Model for Analysis of Competing Hypotheses." Risk Analysis 28, no. 6 (2008): 1699–1709.

Elder, Richard Paul and Linda. The Miniature Guide to Critical Thinking: Concepts & Tools, 2006. http://www.criticalthinking.org/files/Concepts_Tools.pdf.

Ellison, L. "Closing the Credibility Gap: the Prosecutorial Use of Expert Witness Testimony in Sexual Assault Cases." Int'l J. Evidence & Proof 9 (2005): 239.

Elsaesser, Christopher, and Frank J. Stech. "Detecting Deception by Analysis of Competing Hypotheses" (March 25, 2003): 1–7.

Fintzy, R.T. "Criminal Profiling: an Introduction to Behavioral Evidence Analysis." American Journal of Psychiatry 157, no. 9 (2000): 1532–1534.

Foucar, E. "Pathology Expert Witness Testimony and Pathology Practice: a Tale of 2 Standards." Archives of Pathology and Laboratory Medicine 129, no. 10 (2005): 1268–1276.

Frantzen, D. "Interrogation Strategies, Evidence, and the Need for Miranda: a Study of Police Ideologies." Police Practice and Research: An International Journal 11, no. 3 (2010): 227–239.

Fulero, SM. Admissibility of Expert Testimony Based on the Grisso and Gudjonsson Scales in Disputed Confession Cases. 2010 ed. Vol. 38. Journal of Psychiatry & Law, 2010.

Gallini, Brian. "Police 'Science' in the Interrogation Room: Seventy Years of Pseudo-Psychological Interrogation Methods to Obtain Inadmissible Confessions." Social Science Research Network (September 17, 2009).

Garcia Marques, T, and D M Mackie. "Familiarity Impacts Person Perception." European Journal of Social Psychology 37, no. 5 (2007): 839–855.

Garrett, Brandon L. "The Substance of False Confessions." Social Science Research Network (April 2010).

Gould, J B, J Carrano, R. Leo, and J Young. "Predicting Erroneous Convictions: a Social Science Approach to Miscarriages of Justice" (2012).

Heller, K J. "The Cognitive Psychology of Circumstantial Evidence'(2006)." Michigan L Rev 105 (n.d.): 241.

Henry, L., A. Ridley, J. Perry, and L. Crane. "Perceived Credibility and Eyewitness Testimony of Children with Intellectual Disabilities." Journal of Intellectual Disability Research 55, no. 4 (2011): 385–391.

Herman, S. "The Role of Corroborative Evidence in Child Sexual Abuse Evaluations." Journal of Investigative Psychology and Offender Profiling 7, no. 3 (2010): 189–212.

Heuer, Richards J. Psychology of Intelligence Analysis. Center for the Study of Intelligence, 1999.

Heuer, Richards J. "The Evolution of Structured Analytic Techniques." In, 1–9. Washington, 2009. http://www7.nationalacademies.org/bbcss/DNI_Heuer_Text.pdf.

Heuer, Richards J, and Randolph H Pherson. Structured Analytic Techniques: for Intelligence Analysis. Washington: CQ Press, 2011.

Hill, C, A Memon, and P McGeorge. "The Role of Confirmation Bias in Suspect Interviews: a Systematic Evaluation." Legal and Criminological Psychology 13, no. 2 (2008): 357–371.

Houck, Max M, and Jay A Siegel. Fundamentals of Forensic Science. Second Edition. Academic Press, 2010.

Hsu, Spencer S. "Forensic Science Is Not as Dependable as You Might Think" (April 27, 2012).

Jain, Monika. "Mitigating the Dangers of Capital Convictions Based on Eyewitness Testimony Through Treason's Two-Witness Rule." The Journal of Criminal Law and Criminology (1973-) 91, no. 3 (2001): 761–790.

Johnson, P E, S Grazioli, K Jamal, and R Glen Berryman. "Detecting Deception: Adversarial Problem Solving in a Low Base-Rate World." Cognitive Science 25, no. 3 (2001): 355–392.

Josang, Audun, Ansatt, H07. "Plot-Beta-6-2-O3.Ps" (January 4, 2012): 1–69. http://folk.uio.no/josang/papers/subjective_logic.pdf.

Kask, K., and R. Bull. "From Person Descriptions to Interviewing Methods: What Can Be Done to Improve Child Witnesses' testimonies?." Trames 13, no. 63/58 (2009): 2–95.

Kassin, Saul M., Steven A. Drizin, Thomas Grisso, Gisli H. Gudjonsson, Richard A. Leo, and Allison D. Redlich. "Police-Induced Confessions: Risk Factors and Recommendations." Social Science Research Network (July 15, 2009).

Keel, Timothy G, John P Jarvis, and Yvonne E Muirhead. "An Exploratory Analysis of Factors Affecting Homicide Investigations." Homicide Studies 13, no. 1 (2009): 50–68.

Koehler, Jonathan J, Jennifer L Mnookin, Simon A Cole, Itiel E Dror, D Michael Risinger, Jay Siegel, Barry A J Fisher, et al. "The Need for a Research Culture in the Forensic Sciences." SSRN Journal (2011).

Kovera, Margaret Bull. "Microsoft Word - WP Manuscript 08.Doc" (June 6, 2008): 1–109. http://www.ap-ls.org/links/confessions.pdf.

Lassiter, G D, L J Ware, J J Ratcliff, and C R Irvin. "Evidence of the Camera Perspective Bias in Authentic Videotaped Interrogations: Implications for Emerging Reform in the Criminal Justice System." Legal and Criminological Psychology 14, no. 1 (2009): 157–170.

Leo, Richard A., and Deborah Davis. "From False Confession to Wrongful Conviction: Seven Psychological Processes." Social Science Research Network (January 16, 2009).

Leo, Richard A., and Richard J. Ofshe. "The Social Psychology of Police Interrogation: the Theory and Classification of True and False Confessions." Social Science Research Network (June 10, 2008).

Lloyd, C.D., H.J. Clark, and A.E. Forth. "Psychopathy, Expert Testimony, and Indeterminate Sentences: Exploring the Relationship Between Psychopathy Checklist-Revised Testimony and Trial Outcome in Canada." Legal and Criminological Psychology 15, no. 2 (2010): 323–339.

Loewy, Arnold H. "Systemic Changes That Could Reduce the Conviction of the Innocent." SSRN Journal (2006).

Magid, Laurie. "Deceptive Police Interrogation Practices: How Far Is Too Far?." Social Science Research Network (March 2001).

Moore, David T. Critical Thinking and Intelligence Analysis: Occasional Paper Number Fourteen. National Defense Intelligence College, 2007.

National Institute of Justice (U.S.). Technical Working Group on Crime Scene Investigation. Crime Scene Investigation, 2000.

National Institute of Justice (U.S.). Technical Working Group on Crime Scene Investigation. Crime Scene Investigation, 2013.

Oatley, G C, B W Ewart, and J Zeleznikow. "Decision Support Systems for Police: Lessons From the Application of Data Mining Techniques to 'Soft' Forensic Evidence." Artificial Intelligence and Law,(Submitted) (2004).

Paterson, H.M., R.I. Kemp, and J.R. Ng. "Combating Co-Witness Contamination: Attempting to Decrease the Negative Effects of Discussion on Eyewitness Memory." Applied Cognitive Psychology 25, no. 1 (2011): 43–52.

Perron, Brandon A. Uncovering Reasonable Doubt, 1998.

Pherson Associates, LLC. Collaborative Analysis of Competing Hypotheses (C-ACH), 2007.

Pherson Associates, LLC. "Key Assumptions Check" (n.d.): 1–1. http://dungarvanconference.mcintel.net/images/1/18/Packet_-_Key_Assumptions_Check_Description.pdf.

Pherson, Randolph. "The Tradecraft of Warning." Pherson Associates, LLC (February 20, 2009): 1–8.

Pigg, Von H. "Common Analytic Standards: Intelligence Community Directive # 203 and U.S. Marine Corps Intelligence." Small Wars Journal (June 16, 2009): 1–10. http://smallwarsjournal.com/blog/journal/docs-temp/260-pigg.pdf.

Pirrie, Duncan. "Forensic Geology in Serious Crime Investigation." Geology 25, no. 5 (2009): 188–193.

Pope, Simon, and Audun Josang. "Analysis of Competing Hypotheses Using Subjective Logic." In, 1–29, n.d. http://www.cs.umd.edu/hcil/VASTcontest06/paper126.pdf.

Pope, Simon, Audun Josang, and David McAnally. "Formal Methods of Countering Deception and Misperception in Intelligence Analysis" (n.d.): 1–27. http://web.me.com/skjpope/downloads/files/Iccrts-Deception.pdf.

Powell, M B, and R Wright. "Professionals' Perceptions of Electronically Recorded Interviews with Vulnerable Witnesses." Current Issues in Criminal Justice 21, no. 2 (2011): 205–218.

Priehs, Richard Edward. "Abuse of Character Evidence in American Criminal Trials." The Journal of the Institute of Justice & International Studies 17 (2007): 214–230.

Rassin, E. "Blindness to Alternative Scenarios in Evidence Evaluation." Journal of Investigative Psychology and Offender Profiling 7, no. 2 (2010): 153–163.

Rassin, E, A Eerland, and I Kuijpers. "Let's Find the Evidence: an Analogue Study of Confirmation Bias in Criminal Investigations." Journal of Investigative Psychology and Offender Profiling 7, no. 3 (2010): 231–246. http://web.ebscohost.com.ezproxy2.apus.edu/ehost/pdfviewer/pdfviewer?vid=5&hid=122&sid=98e35b4f-e9ee-4ebe-83b1-75331053ce25%40sessionmgr110.

Richards, H J, and R H Pherson. Structured Analytic Techniques for Intelligence Analysis. 2nd ed. Thousand Oaks: CQ Press, 2015.

Shreeve, Thomas W. John O' Malley: an ACH Case Study. Pherson Associates, 2013.

Simon, D. "The Limited Diagnosticity of Criminal Trials." University of Southern California (2011): 72.

Sommoers, Ira B, and Deborah R Baskin. "Crime-Show-Viewing Habits and Public Attitudes Toward Forensic Evidence: the "CSI Effect" Revisited."." Justice System Journal 31 (2010): 97.

Stech, F J, and C Elsässer. "Midway Revisited: Detecting Deception by Analysis of Competing Hypothesis" (2004).

Thomas, David C, and Richard A. Leo. "Interrogating Guilty Suspects: Why Sipowicz Never Has to Admit He Is Wrong by George Thomas." Social Science Research Network (August 27, 2010).

Valtorta, M., J. Dang, H. Goradia, J. Huang, and M. Huhns. "Extending Heuer's Analysis of Competing Hypotheses Method to Support Complex Decision Analysis." Proceedings of the 2005 international conference on intelligence analysis (IA-05)(CDROM), extended version available at http://www. cse. sc. edu/~ mgv/reports/IA-05. pdf (2005).

Weisselberg, Charles D. "Mourning Miranda." Social Science Research Network (February 22, 2008).

Wheaton, Kristan J., Mercyhurst College, and Diane E. Chido. "Structured Analysis of Competing Hypotheses." Competitive Intelligence Magazine 9, no. November-December (2006): 1–4. http://www.mcmanis-monsalve.com/files/publications/intelligence-methodology-1-07-chido.pdf.

Williams, J W. "Interrogating Justice: a Critical Analysis of the Police Interrogation and Its Role in the Criminal Justice Process." Canadian J. Criminology 42 (2000): 209.

Witlin, L. "Mirror-Imaging and Its Dangers." SAIS review (2008).

Notes

Notes

Notes

www.ingramcontent.com/pod-product-compliance
Lightning Source LLC
Chambersburg PA
CBHW081550280526
45788CB00011B/3431